FAUQUIER COUNTY VIRGINIA

Wills, Administrations
and
Marriages

1759-1800

Copyright 1939
By: June Estelle Stewart King

All rights reserved. No part of this publication may be reproduced, stored in a retrieval system, transmitted in any form, posted on to the web in any form or by any means without the prior written permission of the publisher.

Please direct all correspondence and orders to:

www.southernhistoricalpress.com
or
SOUTHERN HISTORICAL PRESS, Inc.
PO BOX 1267
375 West Broad Street
Greenville, SC   29601
southernhistoricalpress@gmail.com

ISBN #0-89308-834-X

Printed in the United States of America

WILLS AND ADMINISTRATIONS

WILL BOOK NUMBER 1

1759 - 1783

BROOKS, WILLIAM
Will dated 10th January, 1767.
To daughter, Sarah, what she has already received from me.
To daughter, Hannah,   "   "   "
To daughter, Danckus,   "   "   "
To daughter, Mary   "   "   "
To daughter, Ann   "   "   "
To daughter, Elizabeth, to have an equal portion with her sisters.
Son, Thomas, to be content with what he has received until decease
of his mother. Son William to have other plantation.
Exrs: William Brooks, Thomas Brooks (sons).
Wit: Peter Conway, George Threkeld. (Page 1)

SMITH, JOHN
Hamilton Parish, Fauquier County. Date of will 3 Sept. 1767.
To sister, Mary Manrony, 160 acres of land in County of Dunmore.
To mother, Jane Smith, land in County of Dunmore; after her decease
land to be divided between sister Hannah Smith and her son, Lewis
Smith. Wit: Augustine Smith, James Smith, William Smith. (Page 2)

BULLITT, BENJAMIN
Inventory. Deceased 9th January, 1767
Apprs: Jonathan Gibson, James Murry, William Ranson. (Page 2)

TULLOS, RICHARD
13 July, 1758.   24 May, 1759.
Peter Lawerence to have all my clothes.
Edward Lawerence, Jr. to have my horse.
To Teanny (or Feanny) Lawerence, money that is now in the hands of
Martin Hmiin; balance of money to her oldest son.
"There is 4£ in the hands of William Stewart that I have no account;
crop at Seaton's to sister's oldest son. Friend, John Markham, to
take charge." Wit: William Marshall, Thomas Conway. (Page 4)

REDMAN, RICHARD
Inventory. 28 June, 1759.   23 August, 1759.
Appraisers: William Underwood, Joseph Smith, Henry Mouffett.
(Page 4)

FOOTE, GEORGE
31 May, 1759.   28 June, 1759.   Hamilton Parish.
To wife, Mary Foote, plantation where I now live, after her decease to
son William, if deceased to son Richard.
To son, Henry Foote, 100 acres of land.
To son, George Foote, 365 acres of land.
To son, Gilson Foote, 640 acres, part of land in Prince William County.
To son, Richard Foote, 556 acres of land.
To son, William Foote, to have plantation at death of mother.
Wife, sons and daughters, Elizabeth, Frances and Bethelon, to have slaves.
Wife and daughters to have household goods.
Sons, Richard and William, to be educated according to satisfaction of wife.
Exrs: wife and sons, George, Gilson, Richard and William.
Wit: William Fletcher, John Burdell, George Russell.   (Page 1)

SHADRACK, JOHN
11 August, 1759.   27 September, 1759.
"Being very sick and weak."
To wife, Elizabeth Shadrack, slaves, household goods and cash.
To Thomas Johnson, who now lives with me, a tract of land in Culpepper
County (640 acres) and his mother's ring that is now in my possession.
Exrs: wife and Charles Morehead (friend).

BRADFORD, WILLIAM
30 September, 1759.   28 February, 1760.
"Very sick and weak in bed."
To son, Henry Bradford, 206 acres of land that I now live on; unborn
child to have one-half of the 206 acres.
To daughter, Ann Bradford, one slave.
Wife, Mary Bradford, to have use of estate, both real and personal.
Exrs: wife and Daniel Bradford (brother).
Wit: Alexander Bradford, Henry Rector, Lazarus Taylor.   (Page 8)

MCCORMICK, JAMES M.
28 June, 1759.   28 June, 1760.   Inventory.
Apprs: John Duncan, Edward Willborn, Francis Tennill.   (Page 9)

HOLTZCLAW, JACOB
Hamilton Parish, Prince William County. 15 January, 1759. 29 February 29,
1760.   To son, Joseph Holtzclaw, 374 acres of land.
To son, Jacob Holtzclaw, 200 acres of land that I purchased of Harman
Kamper and Harmon Button, also land that I purchased of Thomas Barton.
Son, Joseph Holtzclaw, to have the liberty of taking as much timber off
150 acres as he has need for building a dwelling house.
Son, Harman Holtzclaw, to have land that I bought in Prince William
County of Thomas Stone.
Grandsons, Henry and Joseph Holtzclaw, sons of John Holtzclaw (son).
(Continued on page 3)

Grandsons: Henry Hall, Joseph Hall.
To daughter, Eve Wiley (hus. Allen Wiley), 300 acres of land.
To daughter, Elisabeth Miller (hus. Harman Miller), land.
To daughter, Alice Katherine Hitt, 1 Negro boy.
Grandson, Joseph Darnall, son of Jeremiah Darnall, to have 355 acres of land in Prince William County.
Grandson, Jacob Fishback, son of Frederick Fishback, to have 1 Negro.
Land in Augusta County to be sold and the money to be divided among all my children.
Exrs: son Jacob Holtsclaw and Jeremiah Darnall (son-in-law).
Wit: Peter Hitt, Thomas Marshall, Henry Kamper.   (Page 10)

WEAVER, TILLMAN
14 December, 1759. 27 March, 1760.
"Very sick."
Wife, Elizabeth Weaver, to have use of plantation, being land I bought of Martin Hardin and taken up by John Hardin.
After decease of wife land to go to son, Tillman Weaver.
Slaves to be divided between sons Tillman, John and daughter Susannah Weaver. Wife to have livestock.
Daughters: Ann Kemper (hus. John); Mary Hitt (hus. Harman) to have land in Culpepper County and slaves; Eve Porter (hus. Samuel) to have land I bought of Charles Taylor.
Daughter, Elizabeth Weaver, to have 150 acres of land and slaves.
Daughter, Catherine Weaver, to have 150 acres and slaves.
Daughter, Susannah Weaver, to have 89 acres of land and slaves.
Son, John Weaver, to have 150 acres and slaves.
Son, Jacob Weaver, to have 200 acres and slaves.
Exrs: wife, son Jacob, Samuel Porter (son-in-law).
Wit: William Norman, Tillman Martin, Thomas Marshall.   (Page 13)

WRIGHT, JOSEPH
5 November, 1759. 27 March, 1760
Daughters: Hester Jackman, Mary Russell, Catherine Bailey.
Exrs: William Russell, Thomas Jackman.
Wit: Lazarus Taylor, Richard McPherson, Elizabeth Butler.   (Page 14)

TWENTYMEN, EDWARD
12 April, 1759.   22 May, 1760.
Son Benjamin Twentymen, to have 200 acres of land in Prince William County. Son John Twentymen, to have 200 acres on home plantation.
Daughter, Alender Twentymen, to have personal estate.
Wit: William Jett, William Throlkeld and Jesse Threlkeld.
(Page 18)

Inventory of Joseph Wrights estate, 27 November, 1761.
(Page 25)

COOK, JOHN
5 January, 1760.   22 May, 1760
Daughters: Elizabeth Page, Jane Pritchett and Sarah Cook.
Exr: Sarah Cook.
Wit: Isaac Sark, John Loman, William Marshall.   (Page 19)

REDDIN, TIMOTHY
28 August, 1760. Inventory.
Appraisers: Daniel Bradford, Jeremiah Darnall, H. (or A.) Bradford.
(Page 21)

SPILLMAN, JACOB
Sale. 28 August, 1760.   Admr: Daniel Floweree.

CORDER, JOHN
25 September, 1760. Inventory.
Apprs: William Dulin, David Darnall. (Page 24)

BROWN, JOHN
1 October, 1744.   26 February, 1761. Parish of Hamilton, Prince William County. One-half of estate to son, John Brown, and other half to son, Dixon Brown. Personal property to be sold and the money divided among all my children.
Exrs: son John and will
Wit: Lazarus Taylor, William W. Delaney, John Corder.
(Page 28)

ALLEN, JOHN
3 November, 1759.   26 March, 1761
To son, John Allen, land in the Marsh Neck and slaves.
To son, Thomas Allen, all land below Indian Springs.
To son, William Allen, land that I bought from John Hopper, where Gerrard Edwards now lives.
Sons, Joseph and James, to have land on which I now live.
To daughter, Ann Merr (or Marr), 2 slaves.
Exrs: wife and son Thomas.
Wit: George Crump, Benjamin Crump, William McDaniel.
(Page 29)

FINNIE, JOHN
15 August, 1760.   27 November, 1760.
Wife, Ann Finnie, to have all estate during her life time, at her decease estate to be given daughter Hannah.
Exrs: wife, John James (friend).
Wit: Alexander Parker, Daniel Nowlan, Jane Newlan.
(Page 30)

LEGG, DAVENPORT
26 February, 1761. Inventory.
(Page 31)

WYATT, WILLIAM
Inventory. 4 June, 1761.
(Page 37)

BROWN, JOHN
Inventory. 27 August, 1761
Apprs: Alexander Bradford, John Butler, Thomas Smith.
(Page 38)

SMITH, ALEXANDER
Inventory. 26 March, 1761
Apprs: William Reading, David Holder, William Preston.
(Page 39)

OBANNON, BRYAN
4 September, 1760. 23 February, 1762. Hamilton Parish, County of Fauquier. "Sick and weak in body." To son, John Obannon and wife Sarah, land where he now lives, containing 212 acres, and slaves; mention is made of granddau. Sarah, dau. of son John.
To son, William, plantation where he now resides, containing 212 acres.
To son, Samuel, plantation and land in King George County, containing 300 acres, and all wearing apparel.
Daughter, Elizabeth Ambrose, to have 60 pounds of current money and horses. Daughter, Ann Miller, to have 100 pounds of current money.
To grandson, Thomas Obannon, son of John, plantation where I now live, containing 220 acres. Grandson, William Obannon (son of William), to have remaining part of land I now live on. Grandson, Bryan Obannon, son of John, to have slaves. "I give to each of my grandchildren (27 in number) the sum of 10 pounds currency to be paid to them by my executors when they come of age." To Aaron and Francis Johnston, children of Margaret Johnston, my plantation and land in Frederick County. I appoint Jacob Hite (son-in-law) and Elizabeth Hite (gr.dau.) to have care and management of said children until they come of age.
To Aaron Johnston, a slave.
Exrs: sons John and William Obannon and Jacob Hite.
Wit: Elias Edmonds, Samuel Earle, James Rogers. (Page 41)

BEARD, ANDREW
26 November, 1761. 24 September, 1762.
Apprs: Edward Humston, John Ashley, Maxmillian Borryman. (Page 47)

CHURCHILL, JOHN
Bill of sale. 27 August, 1762. (Page 61)

SEAMAN, THOMAS
26 August, 1762. Inventory
Appraisers: E.E.Homo and Martin Hardin.
(Page 56)

BEECH, ALEXANDER
11 March, 1762. ----- No date of probate. Hamilton Parish.
To daughter, Elizabeth Butler, 1 shilling, sterling, with what she is
already possessed with.
Children : Peter Beech, William Beech and Mary Beech, are to each have
1 shilling with what they have already received.
Other children mentioned - Alexander, Thomas and Sarah Beech.
Wife: Margaret Beech.
Exr: John Barber (or Barbee).
Wit: Henry Smith, George Smith, Henry Moseless (,). (Page 63)

STAMPS, THOMAS
8 July, 1761.   26 May, 1763.
To son, Timothy Stamps, 150 acres of land where he now lives.
To son, John, the remaining part of the aforesaid land.
To granddaughter, Molly Stamps (dau. of son Thomas), 15 pounds curr.
To son, William Stamps, ---- not of age.
To son, George Stamps, 150 acres, land that I purchased of Lewis Tackett,
Should son George die before becoming of age, property to go to children
of daughter, Elizabeth Tackett.
Daughter, Elizabeth to receive 10 pounds currency and 800 pounds of
tobacco.   Daughter, Mary Shackleford, to have 10 pounds curr. and 800
pounds of tobacco. Mary Shackleford now has 2 children.
"I lend to wife, Mary Stamps, all moveable estate, both slaves and stock."
Exrs: Timothy, John and William Stamps.
(Pgp 67)

WOODS, ROBERT
Inventory. May 25, 1763
(Page 71)

READING, TIMOTHY
Inventory. May, 1763.
Admr: William Reading.
(Page 72)

HARRILL, JOHN
Administrator of estate Account.
25 February, 1764.
(Page 80)

COPPEDGE, JOHN
Division of the estate of John Coppedge, dec'd. 27 March, 1763.
Elizabeth Coppedge, widow of John, to receive -- 1 Negro man - 50 pounds.
" "   1 Negro boy - 10 pounds.
" "   1 Negro boy - 14 pounds.
William Coppedge, Negroes and 35 pounds curr., John Catlett, guardian.
To Sally Coppedge, 1 Negro girl and 7 pounds and 10 shillings.
To Elizabeth Coppedge, 1 Negro boy and 30 pounds curr.
To John Coppedge, 1 Negro boy and 60 pounds of curr.
Wit: Gilson Foote, James Seaton, James Murray.
(Page 75)

GARNER, JOHN
Inventory, 22 July 1762.
Appraisers: James Arnold, William Morgan, Paul Williams.
(Page 80)

LUTTRELL, RICHARD
27 September, 1764.   25 May, 1766
To son, James Luttrell, 70 acres of land.
To son, Michael Luttrell, 70 acres of land.
To son, Samuel Luttrell, 70 acres of land -- where John Collier formerly lived. Son John to have 70 acres of land.
To son, Richard Luttrell, my new patent of land containing 58 acres.
Land to the following daughters: Unstips (?)Luttrell, Mary Luttrell, and Susannah Luttrell. The last named to have 80 acres of land.
Son Robert to have the place on which I now live, furniture, my new gun, sword and coluck box.
To daughter, Catherine Corum, a tract of land and 5 pounds curr.
To daughter, Sarah Luttrell, a tract of land.
Granddaughter, Mary Corum, to receive 5 pounds curr.
Wife, Mary Luttrell, to have rest of moveable estate in her possession to enjoy during her widowhood.
Exrs: wife and sons Richard and Robert Luttrell.
Wit: Edward Lawrence, Sr., Edward Lawrence, Jr., Richard Lawrence.
(Page 95)

GREEN, DUFF
Inventory. May, 1766.   June, 1766.
Appraisers: John Bell, Wharton Ransdell, H.Brooks.
(Page 100)

DARNALL, MORGAN, JR.
Sept. 30, 1765.   29 July, 1766.
Nun-cupative will.
To brother, Isaac Darnall, land and plantation containing 150 acres,
(Continued on page 8)

horse, bridle, saddle and all wearing apparel.
To brother, Waugh Darnall, 5 pounds due on the rent of my plantation
and all debts due me in Carolina.
To my mother and to my brother Waugh's wife, I give all money in my
pocket book. To John Wood, son of Samuel Wood, as much money out of
my estate that will pay for one year schooling.
To brother John Darnall, rifle gun.
Exr: Morgan Barnall (father).
Wit: Joan Darnall, James Wheakley, Elizabeth Darnall.
(Page 105)

MORGAN, CHARLES, SR.
3 December, 1758. 22 September, 1766. Hamilton Parish. Prince William County.
Seven of my children have received their full parts in proportion of my
estate, both real and personal : Charles, Simon, William, Benjamin, James,
Alice and Mary Morgan.
To "beloved wife", Anne Morgan, 1/3 of my personal estate, the other 2/3
to my son, John Morgan.
Exr: John Morgan (son).
Wit: John Edwards, Garret Edwards and James Edwards.
(Page 107)

BULLITT, BENJAMIN
3 May, 1766. 27 October, 1766.
To son, Joseph, all that id now in his possession and 2 shillings- 6
pence sterling - no more.
To son Thomas Bullitt, a tract of land in the Province of Maryland,
purchased of one Hutcherson, where my father, Joseph Bullitt, was buried.
To daughter, Sith Combs and her husband, John Combs, 1 shilling 6 pence.
To son, Cuthbert Bullitt, 1.shilling 6 pence.
To daughter, Elizabeth Bullitt, slave, silverspoons, feather bed.
To wife Sarah and six sons, slaves.
Names six sons, viz: William Burditt (alias Bullitt), John, George,
Bononi, Parmenas and Burwell Bullitt.
Exrs: wife , sons Thomas and Cuthbert Bullitt,
Wit: Jonathan Gibson, William Connay, Alexander Parker.
(Page 108)

PICKETT, WILLIAM
26 September, 1766. 24 November, 1766.
To daughter, Sarah Pickett, slaves and personal property, when she
comes of age. Wife, Elizabeth Pickett, all estate except land that I
hold in Caroline and Culpepper Counties - to go to son Reuben Pickett
when he comes of age. Land that I hold in Caroline County, after decease of my mother, to be sold and the money arising from sale to be
paid Mary Ann Marshall. Daughter Sarah Pickett to have 70 pounds curr.
After decease of wife property to be sold and divided among 3 sons-
John, Martin and William Pickett, except should my sons George and Reuben Pickett not have as much as the others they shall be made equal.
(Con. page 9)

Exrs: wife and sons. Martin and William Pickett.
Wit: Henry Kamper, James Pony, Philip Kamper, Sarah Pony.
(Page 110)

HAMPTON, RICHARD
24 November, 1766. December, 1766.
Wife, Martha Hampton, to have use of plantation during widowhood.
Daughter, Elizabeth Hampton, to have slaves after decease of wife.
Daughter, Sarah Hampton, to have land and slaves.
Daughter, Martha Hampton, to have 5 slaves.
Sons, William and Richard, to have 5 shillings each.
Grandson, Richard Hampton, after decease of wife to have 2 slaves.
Grandson, Gale Hampton, son of Richard, 1 slave.
Landin Hampshire County to be sold after my decease and widow to pay my debts.
To "my beloved wife" my riding chair and harness.
Exrs: son William and Richard Lingham (son-in-law)
Wit: Charles Morehead, Sarah Sinkler and John Bell.
(Page 112)

SEAMAN, THOMAS (SEAMAN)
Estate Account. 26 May, 1767.
Admr: Martin Hardin.

HOGAN, MARGARET
20 November, 1767. 20 June, 1767
To great-grandchild, Frances Bannister, bed and buggy.
To beloved daughter, Mary Bannister, 1 large chest.
Wit: John Williams, Ann Williams, Frances Moore.
(Page 120)

NEAVILL, JOHN
24 April, 1767. 27 April, 1768.
The following named sons are to receive 1 shilling each: John, Robert, Gabriel and Henry Neavill.
The following named daughters are each to receive 1 shilling each: Milly (?) Fitzgerald, Elizabeth Taylor, Sarah Rodman, Mary Neavill.
Rest of estate to go to son Thomas Neavill.
Exrs: loving friends, George Neavill and John Buchanan.
Wit: James Young, Mary Barratt, Alexander Parker.
(Page 125)

TYLER, MARY
27 August, 1767. Inventory.
Apprs: Thomas Priest, Richard Luttrell, William Ranson.
(Page 126)

DODSON, ABRAHAM
Wfe, Barbarey Dodson, to have slaves, household goods and stock.
Daughter, Milly Holtzclaw, to have slaves, but should she die without
issue then slaves to go to brother Jodeph.
To Tabitha Dodson, slaves.
To son, Enoch Dodson, slaves.
To son, Greenham Dodson, slaves.
To son, Grantham or GrantHano, slaves.
Exrs: wife and Jacob Holtzclaw.
Wit: Absalom Cornelia, Elijah Dodson, John Bennett.
(Page 135)

MOREHEAD, JOHN
23 June, 1768. 24 October, 1768
The following named children are to have 5 shillings over and above
what they have already received: Hannah Johnson, Charles Morehead,
John Morehead, Mary Lawerence and Elizabeth Bristraw (?).
Son, Alexander Morehead, to have 2 slaves.
Son, William to have 15 pounds over and above what he has received.
Son, Samuel, to have a tract of land, containing 90 acres and 50 acres.
The land that wife now lives on to be divided between Alexander, William
and Dressley.
Exrs: sons Charles, Alexander and William.
Wit: John Jett, William Macklin, Joseph Macklan.
(Page 136)

DAVIS, THOMAS
Inventory. November 28, 1768.
Apprs: Stephen McCormack, John Freeman, John Bell.
(Page 139)

MATHIS, ROBERT
30 November, 1766. 23 February, 1767.
To wife, Elizabeth Mathis, land held by lease from Rev. William Stewart
of Stafford County, and slaves.
To son, John Dudley Mathis, land in Prince William County, left by brother, Griffin Mathis.
To son, Chichester Mathis, land purchased of Benjamin Morris in Fauquier
County. Following children to have 1 slave each :- Robert, Alice and
Sarah Mathis.
The 3 youngest daughters: Elizabeth, Ann and Nancy Mathis.
Exrs: wife, James Lane, Newman Mathis.
Wit: Cornelius Kinchloe, James Hamrick, Macmillian Haynie.

MAUZY, MARY
10 February, 1769. 25 September, 1769.
To daughter Sally, slaves and cash.   Brothers: John and Peter Mauzy.
Exr: Thomas Conway (uncle).
Wit: Susannah Kenner, Betty Ranson, J.W.Markham. (Page 152)

MILLER, SIMON
26 March, 1769. 26 February, 1770
To granddaughter, Ann Edmonds, 1 tract of land and household goods.
To granddaughter, Betty Edmonds, tract of land, slaves, copper still, worm and casks.
To granddau. Judith Edmonds, place where George Ford is overseer.
To grandson, Elias Edmonds, 200 acres of land in King George County and slaves.
To brother John, wearing apparel.
To John Hughes, 100 pounds of curr. money the day she marries or when she reaches the age of 18 years.
Exrs: Elias Edmonds, William Edmonds, John Obannon, George Bennett.
Wit: James Craig, Thomas Mackio, Robert Scott.
(Page 155)

BURGESS, FRANCIS
15 Nov. 1767. 20 March, 1770
Wife Jane to have use of entire estate during her life.
To daughters, Jane, Ruth and Ann Burgess, personal estate.
Eleanor Elliott (hus. William) to have 20 shillings to buy a gold ring-no more as she has received her share.
To son Dawson Burgess, lease of land where I now live and slaves.
Granddaughters, Sarah and Ann Elliott, to have household goods.
Exrs: John Suddoth and Francis Tupman (friends)
Wit: Thomas Marshall, John Southard, Benjamin Elliott, Moses Congrove. (Page 157)

WATTS, FRANCIS
23 October, 1753. 28 October, 1769. Of Craven County, South Carolina.
Wife, Ann Watts, to have use of slaves and land during her life, after her decease to grandson, Francis Watts.
Mention is made of other grandchildren, but they are not named.
Exr: wife, but should she die then Benjamin Stone is to act as executor.
Wit: John Dugan, Benjamin Stone, Ann Dargan or Dugan.
(John Watts ordered the above will recorded in Fauquier County.)
(Page 159)

WHITE, PLEASANT
Inventory. 28 May, 1776.
(Page 164)

FOOTE, GILSON
22 October, 1770. Inventory.
Apprs: Richard Foote, Jr., William Alexander, Lynaugh Holm.

SINCLEARE, JOHN
21 June, 1767. 22 April 1771.
Sons William and John to have slaves. Son James to have 213 acres. (Con.)

To son, Robert, slaves and furniture.
To son, Daniel, slaves and furniture.
To daughter, Charity Sincleare, household goods.
To daughter, Jimime Sincleare, feather bed, furniture and 5 pounds curr.
All rest of estate to be divided between five daughters: Sarah, Mary, Elizabeth, Charity and Jimime.
Exrs: sons John and William Sincleare.
Wit: John Wright, John Kerrs (or Kerns), William Preston. (Page 176)

EDRINGTON, JOHN
Inventory. 27 May, 1771.
Apprs: Charles Deane, Thomas King, William Pearse. (Page 179)

BAILEY, CARR
7 October, 1770. 28 May, 1771.
To wife, Mary Bailey, estate during her life or widowhood, after her decease or mariage the estate to be sold and divided among children James, Joseph, Betty, Carr, William and John.
Exrs: George Rogers, Joseph Minters, Jr.
Wit: Humphrey Brooks, William Hampton, Charles Morehead, Thomas Bailey.
(Page 181)

CUMMINGS, SIMON
12 April, 1771. 24 June, 1771.
To son, Alexander Cummings, plantation.
Wife to have use of plantation during her life.
To son, John Cummings, live stock.
To daughter, Sarah Mycratt, stock.
To daughter, Sinty Edge, stock.
To daughter, Conty Birciram, personalty.
Son Peter and daughter Elizabeth Cummings.
Exrs: wife (not named), sons John and Alexander.
        Wit: Daniel Harrilland John Edge. (Page 182)

DARNALL, WILLIAM
28 August, 1771. 23 September, 1771
To Hannah Sears (or Lears), 10 pounds curr, saddle and bridle.
To Sallie Rile, 10 pounds curr.
Exr: Edward Ball
Wit: Sarah Jeffers, Alec Robertson. (Page 187)

STAMPS, WILLIAM
23 April, 1772. 23 March, 1772
Wife ann to have use of estate during life, should she remarry the estate to be divided between children, including unborn child (children not named). Exrs: William Hunton, Robert Sanders.
Wit: Richard Chichester, Peter Hedengran, Margaret Metcalf.
(Page 189)

BOGGS, THOMAS
11 December, 1772. 23 May, 1772
Wife, Hannah Boggs, to have use of estate during her life time.
Sons, Richard, Thomas and Jeromiah Boggs, to have slaves.
Daughters: Magdalen Jackson, Elizabeth Maddox, Hannah Russ Watts, to have slaves. Estate to be equally divided among four youngest children after decease of wife.
Wit: Moses Johnson, Betty Johnson, Eli Edmonds.   (Page 197)

HITT, PETER
23 March, 1772.   July 27, 1772.
Wife, Elizabeth Hitt, to have estate during life.
Slaves to sons, John Joseph and Peter Hitt.
Daughter, Mary Rector, 100 acres of land.
To son, Henry Hitt, 100 pounds of curr. money.
Children: John, Joseph, Harmon, Peter and Mary.
Exrs: sons Harmon and Joseph.
Wit: Harmon Rector, Joseph Taylor, John Morgan, Harmon Rector.
(Page 200)

RECTOR, JOHN
5 July, 1772.   22 March, 1772.
Wife, Catherine Rector to have plantation where I now live during her natural life, after her decease it is to be divided between children.
Son Henry to have 224 acres of land.
Sons, Daniel and Charles
Son Jacob to receive slaves.
Son Benjamin to have plantation.
Son Frederick to have slaves.
To grandson, John Rector (son of John), to have land.
To brother, Harmon Rector, land.
After decease of wife household goods to be divided into six parts—
Sons, John, Daniel, Jacob, Charles, Benjamin, Frederick and children of daughter Catherine (dec'd.) and children of daughter Elizabeth. (Divided into 8 parts)   Exrs: wife and son Henry Rector.
Wit: Henry Rector, John Adams, Jacob Fanbeon (?).   (Page 205)

MINTER, JACOB
21 November, 1772. 26 April, 1773.
Wife to have the bed my father gave me and use of 2 slaves.
Son (unnamed) to have schooling and maintained as thought proper by my executors till he come sof age.
Exrs: William Settle and Hannah Minter.
Wit: Francis Bronbaugh, Andrew Anderson, Edward Settle, John Edwards. (P.207)

MORGAN, RANDLE
30 February, 1773.   27 May, 1773.
Wife, Martha Morgan, to have plantation for her natural life, or until her remarriage, at her decease property to youngest son, Randle Morgan, Jr. (Con)

Sons, Abel and Enoch Morgan, to have 10 pounds curr. money.
Abraham Morgan (son-in-law) to have 10 pounds curr. money.
Randlo Morgan, Jr. will be 21 years of age on 5 October, 1777.
Daughters, Mary, Grace (dec'd.), her daughter, Sarah Carpenter, to have sum of 10 pounds curr.
Exrs: sons Abel and Enoch Morgan.
Wit: Michael Hennie and. Nathan Banley (?). (Page 208)

QUARLES, BETTY
9 September, 1773. 22 November, 1773.
To father-in-law, Thomas Harrison, slaves. (Thomas Harrison was stepfather). To Thomas Gibson (son of Jonathan), slaves.
To brother, Benjamin Harrison, slaves - should brother Benjamin die, then property to go to Burr Harrison, son of brother William, and niece Susannah Humstead, slaves. To Benjamin Harrison (brother), Thomas Gibson, Susana Humstead, cattle etc.
To Burr Harrison (son of William) my bay mare.
To sister, Mary Fowkes, a ring.
To my brother John Quarles daughter, Elizabeth Minor Quarles, ring.
To brother, John Quarles, all my ready cash.
Exrs: Jonathan Gibson (friend).
Wit: William Coppedge, John Coppedge, Benjamin. Jones. (Page 220)

STEPHENS, ROBERT
Inventory. 22 November, 1773. (Page 221)

HARRISON, THOMAS
26 September, 1773, 25 Jan. 1774
To son William, 4 Negroes, land to be divided between him and his brother. Burr. To son Thomas, 409 acres, personal property, money, wearing clothes. To son Burr, 480 acres, plantation house, slaves.
Daughter, Susannah Gibson, 5 Negroes, 200 pounds curr. money, looking glass and my cloak. To daughter, Mary Fowkes, 4 Negroes and 150 pounds curr. money. To daughter, Ann Gillison, 2 negroes and 150 pounds curr.
To grandson, Thomas Gibson, plantation.
To grandson, John Gibson, 2 Negroes.
Gr.daughter, Ann Harrison Fowkes, a Negro.
Jonathan Gibson (son-in-law) to have sum of money he is indebted to me - 79 pounds and 5 shillings.
To Chandler Fowkes (son-in-law) to have sums of money I have several times lent to him -- about 70 pounds.
Grandson, Thomas Harrison Fowkes, 1 Negro.
Grandson, Burr Harrison (son of William), 1 Negro.
To son, Burr Harrison, slaves.
Granddaughter, Lucy Harrison (dau. of William), Negro.
Gr.daughter, Ann Grayson Gibson, a Negro.
Gr.son, Catlett Gibson, (Jonathan Catlatt Gibson), a Negro.
To son, Benjamin Harrison, the old plantation that I purchased of my
(Con. on p.15)

father on Cedar Run, also other tracts of land, large number of slaves, household furniture, at his death this property is to descend to three grandsons, Thomas Gibson, Burr Harrison (son of William) and Thomas Fowkes. To friend and nephew, Cuthbert Harrison, 25 shillings to purchase a mourning ring.
To four nieces, Sith Harrison, Frances Harrison, Ann and Sarah Harrison, the sum of 20 shillings to purchase mourning rings.
To sons, William, Thomas and Burr Harrison, all cattle and hogs at the Mountain, also interest in a large number of slaves.
To Jonathan Gibson (son-in-law) one dark horse.
Exrs: William Harrison, Benjamin Harrison (sons) and Jonathan Gibson.
Wit: --- Young, John Peters, John Shumate, Sr., John Coppage.
(Page 231)

OBANNON, JOHN SR.
18 November, 1773. 28 March, 1774
Wife, Sarah Obannon, to have use and benefit of plantation where I now live during her natural life.
To son William land on the east side of Pigginutt Ridge and slaves; mentions a legacy left son William by grandfather, Bryant Obannon, 189 acres of land.
Son James to have a good suit of clothes.
Son Thomas to have a good suit of clothes.
Son Samuel to have a tract of land and slaves.
Son Andrew to have a Negro, in lieu of a legacy left by grandfather Obannon. Son Joseph, to have a Negro boy, in lieu of 50 pound legacy left by grandfather. To son, Bryant, one riding horse.
To son, Benjamin, new saddle and bridle.
To daughter, Sarah Foley, one Negro.
To daughter, Caty Nelson, one Negro.
Son Bryant to have plantation at death of mother.
Exrs: sons William, Samuel and John.
Wit: Thomas Elliott, Benjamin Elliott, John Moffett.
(Page 237)

ASH, FRANCIS
24 September, 1774. 25 April, 1774.
To wife, Elizabeth Ash, Negroes.
To son, George Ash, 11 Negroes.
To son, Francis (eldest surviving son of wife Elizabeth), land, Negroes and blacksmith tools.
To daughter, Dorothy Allsup, Negroes.
To daughter, Elizabeth , slaves.
To son, Uriel Ash, slaves.
To son, Eon, slaves.
To son, Littleton Ash, slaves.
To daughter, Peggy Neaoble (or Neavill), slaves.
Son William and daughter Molly.
Nine children mentioned.
(Continued on page 16)

Exr: Francis Ash (son).
Wit: Robert Ashley, Enoch Ashley, John Adams.

NEAVILL, GEORGE
Wife, Mary Neavill, to have use of land and slaves.
Daughters, Joanna Hathaway and Judith Barrett, to have land and slaves.
Sons-in-law, John Roper (or Roser), Solomon Jones, Ambrose Barrett and James Hathaway, to have mill on Cedar Run.
Daughters, Lucy Calmes, Ann Blackmore, Milly Barrett, Susannah Hampton, Letty Helms, Mary Roser and Betty Jones, to receive slaves.
Dau. Lucy Calmes to have 120 acres of land.
Mention is made of son-in-law, Richard Hampton, (a slave.)
Gr.daughter, Ann Helms, to have 20 pounds curr.
Gr.daughters, Charlotte and Joanna Hampton, slaves.
Gr.sons, George and William Jones, 20 pounds curr.
Gr.son, John Barrett (son of James) 20 pounds curr.
Carpenter shop to sons-in-law.
Exrs: wife , John Roser, Sol Jones, James Hathaway, Ambrose Barnett.
Wit: Richard Chichester, Sarah Chichester, Samuel Pharis, John Shurley.
(Page 250)

SNELLING, BENJAMIN
8 November, 1773. 27 June, 1774.
To wife, Elizabeth Snelling, the use of estate during life.
Son Benjamin, other children mentioned, but not named.
Wit: Daniel Bradford, Alexander Bradford, Edward Humstead.
(Page 253)

MINTOR, JOSEPH
12 December, 1772. 27 June, 1774.
Wife Mary to have use of esate during her life and at her decease it is to be divided between sons John and Joseph and grandson William Mintor (son of Jacob, dec'd.) to have 25 pounds.
Exrs: Joseph Chilton, William Chilton.
Wit: John Chilton, Will Chilton.
(Page 253)

HALL, RICHARD
March 1, 1774. 25 June, 1774.
All Negroes to remain on the plantation of Mrs. Hannah Corbin until my debts are paid. Mention made of land purchased of Richard and William Hampton.
Children: Elisha Hall Corbin, land and Negroes, dau. Martha Corbin lad and Negroes, should they die their share to go to their mother, Mrs. Hannah Corbin. Sister MaryWilliamson to receive legacy, also her son, James Williamson. Nieces: Martha, Mary, Hannah and Elizabeth Williamson (daus. of sister Mary Williamson). Exr: Mrs. Hannah Corbin of Richmond County. Exrs. in Fauquier County: Wharton Ransdell, James Scott, Thomas Marshall, John Chilton.   (Page 257)

BLACKWELL, WILLIAM
20 September, 1772. 26 September, 1774.
Wife, Elisabeth Blackwell, to have use of land and slaves.
Son William to has use of all land that I bought of Alexander Clement, Chris Marr and Thomas Evan.
Children: John, Samuel, William, Joseph, Hannah, Sarah and Lucy.
Exrs: wife, sons John and William.

LAWSON, ANN STEPHEN (?)
1 June, 1774. 28 Nov. 1774.
To brother, Epaphroditus Lawson, all my Negroes
To brother John and wife a suit of mourning.
To loving uncle Joseph Blackwell and Aunt Lucy Blackwell, a suit of mourning. To Cousin Betty Chilton a suit of worked muslin, not quite finished. Cousin Judith Blackwell to have my stone ring.
To cousins, Elizabeth Lawson, Ann Steptoe Lawson, Harry Lawson, Elizabeth Gibson, wearing clothes.
Sister Mary Lawson to have built a a brick wall around the graves of mother and father.
Exr: brother Epaphroditus Lawson.
(Page 268)

PARKER, WILLIAM
3 April 1775. 22 May, 1775.
Brothers, Alexander and Richard Parker.
All estate to be used to maintain father and mother. At their decease the estate to be divided between brother Richard and sisters Ann and Judith Parker.
Exrs: brothers Alexander and Richard Parker.
Wit: James Shackleford, William Allen, William Hardiwien.
(Page 273)

HERMONS, JOHN
5 April, 1775. 22 May 1775.
To son, James Hermons, 5 pounds sterling, to be educated in English school for six years, to receive 1/4 of estate when he comes of age.
Wife, Mary Hermons, bequeathed land.
Daughters, Mary and Susannah, to receive 3 years education in English school.
Exrs: wife, John Kinchloe.
Wit: John Barker, William Kinchloe, John Kinchloe.
(Page 274)

FOOTE, GEORGE
15 July, 1775. 27 July, 1775.
Wife Celia to have 1/3 of estate during life.
Son Richard Helm to have all land.
Daughter, Hester Foote, to have 1/2 of Negroes and chattels.
Unborn child to share in estate.
(Con. On p. 18)

BRAHAN, JOHN
No date of will. Proven 27 November, 1775
Wife, Lettice, to have slaves and proper part of estate.
Son Thomas to have tract of land where I now live.
Sons, John, William and James, to have slaves.
Mention is made of a daughter, but not named.
Exrs: wife and Morris Hansborough.
Wit: Morris Hansborough, John Nelson, Edward Ralls.
(Page 282)

RENNOLDS, JAMES
2 February, 1776. 25 March, 1776.
Wife, Margaret Rennolds, to have entire estate.
Exr: wife
Wit: Edward Settle, Rosanna Settle, Absalom Iles.
(Page 286)

RANSDELL, WILLIAM SR.
3 July, 1776. 29 October, 1776
Wife (not named) to have estate during her life.
To son, Wharton Ransdell, mansion house and plantation.
Sons, Thomas and William, to have remaining part of land. Mill to
be kept for use of plantation and my 3 sons upon tract of land.
Should son Thomas die his part of estate to go to sons Edward and
Chilton.
Exrs: sons, Wharton, Thomas and William Ransdell.
(Page 389)

CORNWELL, PETER
2 June, 1776. 26 August, 1776.
Wife, Sarah Cornwell, to have use of land during life or widowhood.
Daughter Mary to receive personal estate.
Sons, David and Jacob, each to have a horse.
Sons, Simon and Jarvice, each to have a feather bed.
Exrs: wife, son Simon, Mr. William Hunton.
Wit: J. Moffett, John Dugarde, Anne Cockrell.
(Page 293)

SINKLEAR, JOHN
Inventory. 5 August, 1776
Apprs: Rez. Turner, John Adams, John T.P. Chunn. (Page 295)

JAMES, THOMAS
9 April, 1772. 26 February, 1776
Wife, Mary James, to enjoy 1/3 of estate during her natural life and
at her decease the property is to go to my sons, George and James.
Daughters: Molly, Agatha, Margaret and Elisabeth James, to receive
250 pounds of curr. money. Mention is made of land in Spottsylvania
(Con. page 19)

County, house and lot in Fredericksburg purchased of Warner Washington.
Exrs: Charles Bruce, Thomas Hoard, Gerrard Banks, John James (brother).
Wit: James Allen , John James, William Delaney, Benjamin Cramp (Crump?),
J. H. Smith.   (Page 305)

BARBEY, THOMAS
Inventory. 24 February, 1777
Apprs: Garner Burgess, Samuel Luttrell, Matthew Neal. (Page 307)

HALL, RICHARD
Inventory. July, 1774.
Appraisers: Zach Lewis, James Wright, Jeremiah Darnall. (Page 308)

CARVELL, SANFORD
8 April, 1777.   28 July, 1777
Wife, Elisabeth Carvell, during widowhood, to have jointly with Silvester Welch the plantation on which I now live.
Children: Anna, Dempsey, Porter and Sally Carvell.
Exrs: wife and Capt. John Obannon.
Wit: Thomas Bartlett, Silvester Welch, James Bartlett.
(Page 308)

OBANNON, GEORGE
Date of probate 25 August, 1777. (This will was in form of a letter and probated.)
"Dear Mother and Brothers: - I write to let you know that I am in good health, thanks to God for it, hoping this will find you all in health. Remember me to all my friends, not forgetting Cussen Elisabeth Carle - remember - my love to her. I don't expect I shall write any more and this is to let you know that we have been in no battle yet, but we are expecting it every day and night. We are on an island about fifteen miles long and two or three miles wide, and the innamy is all around the iland and we have no way to get off, we must fit our way off. Our men are fighting every day and night. The other night there was a battle at King's Bridge where the town is on the iland. I am in grate hopes I shall see you all again but we expect a battle every day. I am in hopes the town will be burnt in a few days-- the English would have burnt it before this time, but they want it for barracks, but if they don't burn the town we shall.
Now (no) more at present but your dutiful son, George Bannon."
(Oath of James Foley as to writing) (Page 311)

DODSON, GREENHAME
8 October, 1776. 25 August, 1777
To brother, Enoch Dodson, several slaves.
To sister, Tabitha Shumate, 1 Negro.
To sister, Mary Shumate, 15 pounds curr.
Estate to mother, Barbarby Dodson.
(Con. on page 20)

Exrs: William Hunton, Daniel Shumate
Wit: Johnson Owens, Ajah Shirley.
(Page 312)

METCALFE, CHRISTOPHER
Inventory. March Court, 1777
Apprs: James Murray, John Fields, Uriel Crosby.
(Page 316)

WOOD, SAMUEL
Inventory. May Court, 1777
Apprs: Champ Caram, Thomas Railey, James Luttrell.
(Pg. 317)

CHILTON, JOHN
24 August, 1776. 24 November, 1777
Land purchased of Debutts to be sold and the money divided among the children they of age :- Joseph, Lucy, George and Nancy.
Executors to give children such education as the estate will afford.
To son, Thomas, land given me by my father where I have lately lived.
Exrs: Charles Chilton, Major Martin Pickett, Thomas Keith.
Wit: Samuel Boyd, John Blackwell, John Ashby, Jr., Isham Keith, Joseph Blackwell, Jr.   (Page 320)

BULLITT, THOMAS
17 Sept. 1775. 25 Feb. 1778
Executor to build a house for brother Joseph on land where he now lives. And that executor shall carry into execution an agreement made and entered into by me with Cuthbert Combs relative to sundry lands upon Kankawa River at the mouth of the Elk.
To Sarah Bronaunt, 400 acres of land and slaves. To Sarah Bronaunt, natural daughter of Martha Bronaunt, a young Negro wench.
To sister, Sith Combs, 15 pounds to purchase a mourning ring.
To Mr. Benjamin Harrison, 2 colts. To Cuthbert Combs, a horse.
Rest of estate to brother, Cuthbert Bullitt, who is also named as executor. Wit: William Blauset, John Blauset, Charles Grey.   (Page 321)

MINTER, JOHN
Wife Mary to have 1/3 of estate during life or widowhood.
After decease of wife estate to be divided between children, William, Elizabeth and Jacob.   Son Anthony to have a tract of land left me by my father, Joseph Minter, also to have worm and still and a good country education.   Daughter Elizabeth to be raised by sister Rogers..
Exrs: Charles Chilton, Joseph Minter, George Rogers.
Wit: George Rogers, Mary Baley, William Tomlin.
(Page 322)

ETHERINGTON, ELIZABETH
29 November, 1776. 23 March, 1778
To Catherine Nelson, 1 feather bed and personal property.
All "Waring cloathes" to be equally divided between Catherine Nelson and Betty Allen and Catherine Duncan.
To Benjamin Russell, 1 bed and personal property.
To nephew, Thomas Obannon, son of Samuel and Stalle, 1 tan --- (illegible) for use during life and Capt. John Wright to have use of same for life.
Nephew Thomas to have slaves.
Exrs: Elias Edmonds, Sr., Jeremiah Darnall.
Wit: Henry Bramlett, Berryman Jennings, James Wright.
(Page 323)

SHIPP, JOHN
19 February, 1778. 23 March, 1778.
Slaves are bequeathed to daus. Sukey Drummon, Polly Shipp, Nancy Shipp, Nancy Shipp. Sons to receive slaves: Richard Wiatt Shipp, Laban and Colby Shipp.
Exrs: sons Laban and Richard Shipp.
Wit: Thomas Lewis, Thomas James, William Donaldson.   (Page 324)

CATLETT, JOHN
3 February, 1778. 28 March, 1778
To son, John Catlett, 1 shilling.
To son, William Catlett, the plantation where I now live - containing 179 acres. To daughter, Elizabeth Catlett, 2 white boys until they arrive at the age of 21 years, which boys were purchased for me with their father and mother of Mr. Hector Ross and the Indenture taken in the name of Alexander Catlett.
To daughter, Jane Coppage, personalty.
To granddaughter, Margaret Hume, weaving loom and gear belonging to old loom.
To daughter, Bersheba Young, "Furniture and Bed I now ly on."
Remainder of moveable estate to be divided between Mary Ann Hogan, Elizabeth Catlett, Jane Coppage, Bersheba Young, Isabbell Summers and (Frances Priest.)
Exrs: Moses Coppage, John Hogan.
Wit: James Holmes, James Dowdall, Original Young, William Pope. (P.326)

BRONAUGH, JOHN
1 July, 1777. 25 March, 1778. Overwharton Parish, Stafford County.
To beloved wife, Mary Ann, slaves and all estate, provided that she does not remarry. To son William, a tract of land in Prince William County, where lives John Delgram, William Davis, Meredith Moss.
To son John, 500 acres in Loudon County.
Daughter, Margaret Bronaugh, to have slaves. Dau. Mary Mason Bronaugh bequeathed slaves. A tract of land lying in Fairfax County, bequeathed me by my mother, Sympha Rosenfield Bronaugh, to be sold.
Exrs: wife and brother William Bronaugh.
(Page 327)

DONALDSON, STEPHEN
Inventory. 8 August, 1777
Apprs: Painick George, Benjamin Robinson, William Roach.
(Page 329)

DUGARD, JOHN
Inventory. 25 May, 1778
Apprs: William Norris, Rowley Smith, Joseph Taylor.   (Page 331)

JAMES, JOHN
6 November, 1777. 25 May, 1778. Hamilton Parish, Fauquier County.
"Being sick and weak in body."
To son, Thomas James, all that tract of land lying on the easternmost side of Spring Branch, which land came by his mother, as this is a small quantity of acres of land which came by her on the other side of Spring branch, I give to son Thomas in lieu of other land. His mother's land was 500 acres as a whole.
Son Thomas not to possess the land until decease of mother.
To son, Benjamin, plantation where I now live, after decease of mother.
To son, James, a tract of land and slaves.
To daughter, Susannah James, a horse and bridle, personalty.
To granddaughter, Hannah Finnie, bed & furniture, cow & calf.
To grandson, Benjamin James, horse and bridle, furniture etc.
To wife, Dinah James, residue of estate during widowhood, all land not bequeathed to children.
Daughters: Sarah Hitt, Ann Tullis, Hannah Humes, Elizabeth Bradford, Mary Conway, Dinah Thompson, Susannah James.
Exrs: wife and sons, Thomas, Benjamin, John James.
Wit: William Grant, John Kerr, Jonathan (?) Markham, Marmaduke Brown.
(Page 332)

MARR, MARY
Inventory. 4 June, 1776. (Page 334)

LEWIS, SARAH
4 Feb. 1778. 22 June, 1778.   Of Loudon County, Virginia.
To daughter, Silby West, 1 mourning ring.
To daughter, Sarah Manly, 1 mourning ring.
Rest of estate to daughter, Mary Peake, during her life, at her decease to her children.
Exr: John Peake (son-in-law)
Wit: William Whitely, Cleater Smith.
(Page 336)

RUST, JOHN
Inventory. 22 June, 1778.
Apprs: Thomas Nelson, Benjamin Rector, Joseph Robinson.
(Page 337)

CORNWELL, PETER
Inventory. 22 June, 1778
Apprs: Thomas Maddux, Thomas Watts, George Kennard.
(Page 338)

FOOTE, GEORGE (GENTLEMAN)
Inventory. 22 June, 1778.
Apprs: Benjamin Harrison, John James, Jonathan Gibson. (Page 340)

WINN, MINOR
30 July, 1775. 23 March, 1778.
To son, William Winn, a slave.
To granddaughter, Martha Smith, a slave.
To son, James Winn, a slave.
To son, Minor Winn, my Great Bible, personalty, etc.
To son, Richard Winn, slaves.
To daughter, Margaret Johnson, slaves.
To daughter, Mary Smith, slaves.
To daughter, Susan Grant, slave.
Forty pounds to be divided between children of daughter, Elizabeth Smith.
Exrs: wife Margaret Winn, son Minor Winn.
Wit: Stephen Tolle, Thomas White, James Fleming. (Page 343)

JENNINGS, AUGUSTINE
13 December, 1776. 24 August, 1778. Of Hamilton Parish.
Wife, Hannah Jennings, to have plantation during life.
Son, William Jennings, to have 200 acres of land and all goods and chattells that he has received.
The following named sons are to receive land and slaves: Benjamin, Baylor, George, Berryman, Lewis and Augustin.
Daughter, Betty Jennings, to have 40 pounds curr. money.
To daughter, Hannah, slaves.
  To daughter, Sally, 2 slaves.
To daughter, Jemina Hudnall, all estate that she has received.
To daughter, Fanny Obannon, 1 slave and all estate she has received.
To daughter, Nancy Weathers, 1 slave. and 10 pounds curr.
To daughter, Cloe Weather, 1 slave
Exrs: sons , Augustin and William Jennings.
Wit: Henry Bramlett, Peter Barker, Lucretia Russell. (Page 346)

LUTTRELL, MICHAEL
16 March, 1776. 24 August, 1778.
To daughter, Franklin McKenzey, large pot.
To dau. Hannah Luttrell, 1 bed & furniture.
To son Abner, 1 sorrel horse.
To daughter Lydia, 1 bed & furniture.
To son Michael, 1 pair of stillards.
To son Nathan, bell metal skillet.
To daughter, Dinah Luttrell, 30 weight of feathers.
(Con. on page 24)

To son Nathan, a Bell metal skillet.
To son Richard, 1 hand saw.
To daughter Sarah, 1 large and 1 small Pewter Basons.
To daughter Dolly, black walnut chest.
To son Lot, 120 acres of land.
To daughter Mary, 1 sugar bowl.
To daughter Betty, my trunk.
To wife, Dinah Luttrell, all moveable estate to be by her possessed and enjoyed during her natural life and then divided among all my children.
Exrs: wife, Richard Luttrell, John Luttrell.
Wit: John Combs, Richard Coram, Robert Luttrell.
(Page 351)

WEBB, JOHN
Inventory. 24 August, 1778.
Admrtx: Mrs. Judith Webb.
Apprs: John Adams, Thomas Chunn, John Ashby.

WEBB, JOHN
4 February, 1777. 23 May, 1778
Wife, Judith Webb, to have land and slaves during her life.
Sons, John and William, to have slaves.
Slaves to daughter, Priscilla Webb.
A tract of land in Northumberland County bequeathed to wife.
Exrs: wife, William Ballard, William Miskel, John Keith.
Wit: John Keith, James Keys. (Page 355)

KENNER, HOWSON
9 April, 1778. 28 Sept. 1778
To oldest son, Francis Kenner, all money in hands of my son-in-law, William Seaton, but 40 pounds, the balance of the money said Seaton owes me (210 pounds) for the 250 acres of land (250 acres) which I sold to him.
To daughter, Betty Seaton, 20 pounds.
To daughter, Rebecca Clifton, 10 pounds - no more.
To daughter, Mary Seaton, 10 pounds - no more.
To son, George Turville Kenner, a tract of land and slaves.
To grandson, Rodham Kenner (son of George) a tract of land.
To daughter, Peggy and husband, Stephen Prichard, a slave & 20 pounds.
To grandson, Howson Kenner, (son of Francis).20 pounds.
To son, Rodham, tract of land that I now live on and 20 pounds curr.
Grandson, George Seaton, 10 pounds - no more.
To daughter, Catoy Markham- and her daughter Mary Ann, slaves and live stock. Gr.son, Samuel Eskridge, alias Kenner, son of dau. Susannah, 2 slaves and 100 pounds cash with which to educate him.
Exrs: Mr. Joseph Blackwell and daughter Susannah.
Wit: Original Young, William Pope.
(Page 358)

HAMBUCKS, JAMES
Inventory. 23 November, 1778
Apprs: John Morehead, Peter Laurance, John Southard. (Page 361)

STROTHERS, JAMES, SR.
28 Sept. 1778. Inventory.
Apprs: William Kinchloe, Harman Hitt, John Hathaway. (Page 361)

ELLIS, JOHN
3 December, 1778. 22 Feb. 1779. Parish of Leeds. Fauquier County.
To daughter, Ann Ellis, household goods.
To son, Jonathan Ellis; 8 hogs.
Rest of estate to my 2 youngest sons, Owen and William Ellis.
Exr: son Jonathan Ellis.
Wit: Berry Neale, John Robertson, James Robertson.
(Page 368)

MARTIN, TILMAN
23 May, 1778. 26 July, 1779
"Sick and Weak." To wife, Elizabeth Martin, live stock and land, which she may sell when she thinks proper and money to be used to purchase another place, which place is to be for my son, Tilman Martin, should he die it is to go to youngest son (unnamed).
To daughter, Elinor Martin, mare colt etc
Exrs: wife, son Elijah Darnall.
Wit: Jeremiah Darnall, Thomas Parker, John Parker. (Page 377)

PRICE, BENNETT
9 July, 1774. 24 October, 1774. Parish of Hamilton.
To loving wife, Judith Price, lands.
Daughters: Elizabeth, Ann, Judith.
Exrs: wife, Martin Pickett, William Edmonds, Armistead Churchill.
Wit: Martin Pickett, Joseph Blackwell, Jr., Samuel Blackwell, Jr.,
Ann Pickett. (Page 378)

GEORGE, NICHOLAS
24 June, 1779. 27 September, 1779.
Wife, Margaret George, to have estate during her life, at her decease it is to be divided among following named children: Nicholas George (eldest son) to have slaves.
Son William, slaves.
To son, Joseph, livestock and slaves.
Daughters, Elizabeth, Lydia and Wilmouth to receive slaves.
Exrs: wife, sons Joseph and William George.
Wit: John Nelson, Thomas Tidler (?).
(Page 380)

BAILEY, JOHN
8 Sept. 1778. 27 Sept. 1779
To son, Wright Bailey, land and personal estate.
Exrs: Charles Morehead, Thomas Morehead.
Wit: Charles Turner, Mary Morehead.
(Page 381)

BEACH, PETER
2 April, 1777. 25 October, 1779
To son, John Beach, a tract of land.
To grandson, John Baker, a tract of land in Fincastle County (Va.).
Daughters, Mary, Sarah, Lettice, Ann Beach to have 30 pounds cash, live stock and slaves.
Exrs: Samuel Baker (son-in-law), William Butler.
Wit: Peter Conway, William Butler.
(Page 383)

SOUTHARD, FRANCIS
20 Oct. 1779. 22 November, 1779.
To wife, Elizabeth Southard, a tract of land during her life, at her decease to son Levi.
To son William, feather bed and furniture.
To son, George, a mare.
To daughter, Sarah Dodds, 3 sheep.
To daughter, Jemina, feather bed & furniture.
Exrs: wife and James Duff.
(Page 384)

SCOTT, JAMES
2 January, 1779. 22 November, 1779. Of Parish of Leeds.
To wife, Elizabeth Scott, whole of estate during widowhood; mentions land in Prince William County and on the Ohio river.
Daughters: Sarah, Frances, Elizabeth and Nancy Scott.
Sons: Alexander, James, Cuthbert and Thomas Scott.
Exrs: wife, Cuthbert Bullitt, Cuthbert Harrison.
Wit: James Stewart, Samuel Boyd, William Stewart. (Page 385)

SIAS, JOHN
6 Sept. 1773. 22 Sept. 1779.
Wife to have full maintenance out of estate.
Daughter, Mary Hamrick, to have 5 pounds curr. money.
To Thomas Chapman, land and slaves.
Exrs: Thomas Chapman, William Carr.
Wit: James Marshall, James Guthrie, John Tebbs. (Page 386)

BARHAN, PETER
6 Nov. 1779. 27 March, 1780
To wife, Celia Barhan, whole estate during widowhood, should she
(Con. on page 27)

remarry to have 1/3 of estate.
To son, Peter Barhan, slaves and land in Fauquier County.
Children: Molly, Rawleigh Chinn, Elijah, Betsy and Sukey Barhan.
Exrs: wife, Charles Chilton.
Wit: John Norris, Joseph Taylor, John Coppedge.
(Page 387)

FOOTE, RICHARD
24 February, 1779. 24 April, 1780. Of Stafford County.
To brother, William Foote, whole of estate.
Wit: William Lawerence, Lawerence Washington.
(Page 389)

TOLLE, ROGER
2 Feb. 1778. 22 May, 1780
Wife, Sarry Tolle.
To sons, Roger and George, 5 pounds each.
To granddaughter, Susannah (dau. of Jonathan), 5 pounds cash.
Children: Jonathan, Ann Squires, Roger, James and Stephen.
Exrs: wife, sons Roger and Stephen Tolle.
Wit: Edward Turner, Mary Turner, Elisabeth Grogan.
(Page 390)

ARNOLD, JOHN
7 September, 1771. 22 May, 1780.
To son Benjamin, 100 acres – where I now live.
Wife to have stock and household goods.
Admr: Benjamin Arnold.
Wit: William Settle, Edward Settle, John Edwards
(Page 391)

PEAKES, JOHN
8 June, 1779. 22 May, 1780. Of Hamilton Parish.
To wife, Mary Peake, all property to dispose of at her discretion.
To daughters, Sally, Mary, Elizabeth Peake, slaves.
To son, Thomas Peake, slaves.
Exr: wife
Wit: John Carvell, Judith Carvell.

FEAGIN, EDWARD
8 July, 1778. 24 July, 1780
To wife, Elizabeth Feagin, to have estate for life, at her decease
to be divided among my nine children: John, Edward, William, Elizabeth,
Sarah, Susannah, Cleary, Mary and Frances.
Wit: Evan Griffith, James Thomson Clark, Charles Chadduck.
(Page 398)

KIRK, WILLIAM
1 May, 1779. 27 November, 1780
Should he die without children, the estae to be sold and money sent to relatives in Scotland, John McIoar, James McIoar, Mary McIoar and Elizabeth McIoar, children of John McIoar' and Sarah Kirks.
To wife, Elizabeth Kirk, 1/2 personal estate and slaves.
Exrs: David Allison, William Allison, Gavin Lawson (of Culpepper Co.)
Wit: William Pickett, James Bell, John Peake, Jr., Charles Morehead, Presley Morehead, William Hinton.
(Page 409)

ELLIOTT, REUBEN
29 July 1779. 27 November, 1780
Wife, Ruth Elliott, to have possession of estate to keep younger children. William Cundiffe alias Elliott, 100 acres of land and wearing apparel. To son, Reuben Elliott, slaves and personal property. To son, Thomas Elliott, slaves and personal property.
Children: Reuben, Thomas, Anne Roberson, Elisabeth, Mildred, Jemina and Molly Elliott.
Exrs: wife, with her son, William Cundiffe - Elliott and John Obannon.
Wit: John Hathaway, William Peake, John Barker, Daniel Morrison.
(Page 410)

PRIEST, WILLIAM
5 March, 1781. 28 May 1781
To wife, Eveles (?) Priest, and Samuel Priest, 5 pounds of curr. to be divided between them.
To brother, John Priest, bed, bed stead, furniture, all woolen clothes, all linen clothes, except 7 yards of linen I leave to my loving mother, Sary Priest. To "loving" brother, Thomas Priest, a slave.
To sister, Sary Murry (?), chest, chairs, what pewter I have.
To brother, George Priest, 34 bushels of corn.
To brother, Richard Priest, a cow.
To sister, Elizabeth Stark, 1 horse, all cash I have and 544 pounds of tobacco. Exrs: Thomas Priest (brother), James Stark.
Wit: James Peters, James Darnall, James Stark.
(Page 415)

ADAMS, JOHN
14 January, 1780. 28 May, 1781
"Weak of body." To son John, all land in Maryland.
To son, George, land on which I now live.
To daughter, Elizabeth, 300 acres of land where she now lives.
To dau. Susannah, 300 acres of land where James Hume now lives.
To son, Josias, all land I purchased of Capt. Turner.
To wife, Sarah Stacy, to have remainder for life or widowhood.
Wit: Hezekiah Turner, John Hickman, John Chinn, Will Bailes (Bailes).
(Page 416)

COMBS, JOHN, JR.
7 October, 1780. 28 May, 1781. Nuncupative Will.
Estate to be divided between 2 sons and 4 daughters--
Nimrod Combs, alias Luttrell; John Combs; Nannie Combs, alias Luttrell; Bethaland Combs, alias Luttrell; Betty Combs; Heland Combs, alias Luttrell; Sarah Combs. Proven by oath of Original Young and Evis Combs.
(Page 416)

FOWKES, GERRARD
July 26, 1781. Division of estate. (Page 419)

GRIGSBY, SAMUEL
11 May, 1781. 22 Oct. 1781. Parish of Leeds.
To wife, Ann Grigsby, estate during her widowhood. Should she remarry estate to be sold and divided among the children.
Mentions mother, Mrs. Dade, of Prince George County, Virginia.
Exrs: Henry Peyton, William Grigsby, James Grigsby.
Wit: John Scott, John Fishback, Peter Tait.
(Page 420)

PETERS, JOHN
4 October, 1781. -----
To wife (unnnamed) to have dwelling house, land and slaves, during widowhood.
To son, John Peters, land and slaves.
To sons, Nimrod and James Peters, parcel of land in Stafford County that I purchased of James Peters- 413 acres and slaves.
Nimrod to have 1/6 part of my land in Caintucky.
Son, James Peters, part of land in Caintucky and slaves.
To my two sons, Lewis and William, land on which I now live, after decease of my wife.
Daughters, Nancy, Sarah, Betty, a slave each.
Exrs: wife, John Ashby, John Peters, Joseph Combs, Cuthbert Combs.
(Page 423)

BROWN, CHARLES
22 October, 1781. Inventory.
(Page 422)

STEWART, JAMES
26 May, 1781. 22 October, 1781. Hamilton Parish.
To wife, the moiety of a tract of land that I purchased of Richard Grubbs, whereon my son John now lives, to have during her natural life, at her decease to son John. "Beloved" wife to have 2 cows, 2 ewes, 2 sows with pigs, feather bed, dishes and choice of horses.
To son Allen, a Negro lad named Solomon, feather bed, cow & calf.
To son, William, 14 pounds in gold or silver.
To son, James, 10 pounds in gold or silver.
Son Charles has been provided for and he is not to possess any more

of my estate. After my decease certain negroes are to be sold and all remainder of my estate, except what has been given or lent my wife, out of which above mentioned legacies to sons William and James are to be paid, remainder to daughters, Mary, Betty, Jane and Helen. All articles lent wife to be sold at her decease and divided between daughters.
Exrs: wife, son James and James Hathaway.
Wit: William Metcalfe, Betsy Metcalfe, Sarah Elliott. (Page 424)
(Name of wife not given in will, but it was Jane Stewart.)

FOWKES, ELIZABETH
20 June, 1781.   22 Oct. 1781
To son, George Fowkes, a tract of land and slaves, should he die land to go to son William Fowkes.
Daughters, Mary and Enfiets (?) shall be in possession of dwelling house while they are single. All slaves to be divided among all children. Children: William, Mary, Chandler, Enfiets(?), George, Elizabeth Phillips.
Wit: Willy Roy, William Wright, Joshua Butler, Joseph Morgan. (Page 426)

RECTOR, HENRY
April 2, 1781.   26 Nov. 1781
Wife mentioned, but not named.
To son, William Rector, land that Capt. William Smith now lives on.
To son, John Rector, slaves, tract of land and part of moveable estate.
To son, Enoch Rector, slave and 150 acres of land.
Exrs: Benjamin Rector (brother), Frederick Rector:
Wit: Harman Rector, Jr., Harman Rector, Sr., Henry Utterback.
(Page 427)

SETTLE, WILLIAM
5 February, 1782.   25 March 1782.
To wife, Sarah, estate during widowhood, afterwards to be divided between sons, Edward, Pope Williams, William Freeman.
To daughter, Elizabeth Settle, 100 acres of land, household goods and slaves.   To son, William Freeman, 100 acres of land.
To son, Edward, 550 acres of land.
Exrs: sons Edward and William Freeman.
Wit: John Spillman, Nancy Settle, Henry Settle, Francis Sudduth, Benjamin Arnold. (Page 428)

JACKMAN, THOMAS
15 March, 1776.   25 March, 1782.
To son, Thomas, 130 acres of land, he is to pay Betty Stone 50 shillings for it.   To son, Richard, 130 acres of Pigmit Bridge tract, he is to pay my daughter, Sarah Neavill, 50 shillings for it.
To son, Adam, old plantation, he is to pay Maragret Underwood 50 shillings for it.
(Con. on page 31)

To son, William, 100 acres where he now lives.
To son, Joseph -----
Daughters, Rebecca Smith and Hannah Smith, a slave each.
Exrs: Thomas, Richard, Adam Jackman (sons).
Wit: Thomas James, John Johnson, Henry Moffett, Jr. (Page 430)

NEWELL, BENJAMIN
2 Oct. 1780. 25 March, 1782
Legatees: Ann Wheatley, Leannah Wheatley, Sarah Wheatley (all of Fauquier County), each to have a gold ring of 20 shillings valuation. To beloved John Newell (son of bro. Richard), 400 pounds of curr. money. To sister Nancy Newell, balance of estate.
Wit: Samuel Holiday, James Dobie.
(Page 432)

HOLTON, ALEXANDER
5 March, 1782. 25 March, 1782.
Wife, Elizabeth Holton.
Exr: son William
Wit: John Monroe, Lewis Woodyard, Henry Ford. (Page 433)

MILLARD, WILLIAM
4 January, 1782. 25 March, 1782.
Land to wife (not named), should she remarry all estate to Thomas Cummings. Thomas Cummings to have all wearing apparel.
Legatees: Ann Sudduth, wife of John Sudduth.
Exrs: wife, James Thompson, Original Young.
Wit: Richard Coram, Champ Coram, John Cummings.
(Page 433)

SMITH, MATHEW
25 November, 1781. 25 March 1782.
Wife, Martha Smith, to have use of estate during widowhood.
To son, William Smith, a gun.
To sons, Joseph and James, a horse each.
Exrs: wife, James Smith (brother), Minor Winn.
Wit: Thomas Smith, Joseph Smith, James Key. (Page 434)

COOK, LITTLETON
28 February, 1782. 22 April 1782
To brother Giles Cook, horse and bridle and 1/2 of clothes.
To brother, Thomas Cook, remainder of estate.
Exrs: Richard Willis.
Wit: Francis Whiting, Betty Whiting. (Page 437)

ROBINSON, JOSEPH
21 May 1782. 22 July, 1782. (Con. on page 32)

Wife, Martha, to have land a d slaves during widowhood, at her decease
estate to be equally divided among all children.
Children: Maxmillian, John, William, Dorcas Murry, Hannah Kinchloe,
Catherine Robinson, Peggy Robinson, Molly Robinson.
To grandson, Maxmillian, 10 pounds curr. money.
To gr.daughter, Hannah Robinson, 10 pounds curr.
To gr. daughter, Lucy Robinson, 10 pounds curr. (The last 3 mentioned
grandchildren were children of Berryman Robinson, dec'd).
Exrs: wife and son John.
Wit: John Barker, Joseph Robinson, Jesse Robinson, James Wright.
(Page 445).

KINCEFORD, GEORGE
21 July, 1781. Inventory.
Apprs: Charles Morehead, Turner Morehead, Moses Bailey.
(Page 446)

HULETT, LEROY
26 August, 1782. Inventory.
Wit: Thomas Payne, Josias Bayse, B.Piper.

BLAND, MARY
3 August, 1782. 28 Oct. 1782.
To son, Charles Bland, a tract of land I bought of William Sanford
Pickett. To son, Jacky Bland (youngest son), a slave.
To daughter, Betty Bland (youngest dau.), a slave.
Eldest son, James Bland. Eldest daughter, Esther Bland, to have 1
shilling. To daughters, Peggy Mooboy, Chloe Pitcher, Amelia Brady, a
shilling each.
Exrs: Charles Metcalfe, John Mumney. (Page 450)

SEATON, WILLIAM
8 May, 1782. -----
Each daughter at marriage to receive from their mother, household goods.
Sons: James and William Seaton.
Exrs: wife, Rodham Kenner, William Con way.
Wit: George Marshall, Robert Kenner, George Turberville, David Wick-
liffe. (Page 452)

FIELDS, DANIEL
27 July, 1777. 24 March, 1783.
To sons, George, Lewis, John and Fielden Fields, slaves.
Wife's dower to be divided among surviving children.
Daughters: Ann, Hannah, Sarah, Elizabeth, Mary and Milly.
Granddaughter, Charlotte Haddocks.
Exrs: friend Daniel Fields, of Culpepper County.
(Page 458)

FURR, THOMAS
20 July, 1777. 25 March, 1783.
Thomas Furr alias Johnson.
To loving wife, Elizabeth Furr, horse, saddle and furniture.
To Benjamin Williams, horse, saddle and bridle.
To Thomas Cummings (cousin) 10 pounds curr.
To Thomas Foyer (?), son of Moses, 10 pounds curr.
Exrs: wife, Thomas Cummings.
Wit: W. Waller, Ann Conway, William Smith, Ann McChesney.
(Page 460)

BALL, CAPT. WILLIAM
Inventory. 10 November, 1772   (Page 467)

JOHNSON, JEFFREY
11 June, 1782. 26 May, 1783
Son, Alexander, to have tract of land.
To wife, Sarah, land and rest of estate for life.
Sons, Bailey, Alexander, James and Presley.
Son Presley to have a tract of land.
Daghters: Mary Cockrell, Elizabeth Morris, Sarah Johnson, Elizabeth Johnson.
Exrs: sons Bailey and Alexander.
Wit: Anderson Cockrell, Jesse Moffett, John Monroe.   (Page 469)

ROPER, JOHN
6 April, 1783. 23 June, 1783
Sons, Richard and John to have land in Rappahannock County.
Sons John and William to have land where I now live.
Daughters: Nancy, Sarah, Sukey, Violet, Letty, Winny, Sally, Elizabeth have received their share of estate. (Page 473)

MADDUX, THOMAS
15 October, 1782. 23 June, 1783.
To wife, Margaret, all personal estate, tract of land in Prince William County, containing 260 acres.
Daughter, Easter Sally Maddux, horse & saddle.
Daughter, Fanny, to have furniture.
Daughter, Darkes Jones, to have furniture.
One shillings each to following named sons: Thomas, Mathew (or Martin), Lazarus, William, Nathaniel and Jethrofield.
Exrs: wife and son Lazarus. (Page 476)

MURRY, JAMES
29 March, 1783. 28 July, 1783.
Wife, Lydia, to have use of land during life. Land to son Ralph and John Seaton (son-in-law). Exrs: sons, Ralph, John, Reuben.
Wit: John Butler, Nathan Cockran, Daniel French.

BRADFORD, MARY
6 July, 1775. July 1783
To daughter, Sarah Rose, saddle.
Wearing apparel to be divided among three daughters.
Granddau. Ann Fowler. Exrs: sons Alexander and Benjamin Bradford.
(Page 480)

MAUZY, JOHN
20 February, 1764. 26 July, 1764.
To loving wife, Betty, 7 slaves and land where I now live, during widowhood. Daughter, Peggy, to have slaves.
Should above heirs die then estate to go to daughter, Margaret.
To dau. Molly, 226 acres of land in Culpepper County; 300 acres of land 15 miles from Winchester. slaves, my property for which I have sued Jonathan Perkins for in chancery, at my death suit is to be renewed. To daughter, Betty, 163 acres of land which I purchased of Robert Jackson in Frederick County and 198 acres in Hampshire County. Mentions nephews, John, Henry and William Rousan.
Exrs: wife, Henry Mauzy (brother), Peter Mauzy and William Rousan.
Wit: Thomas Conway, John Edge, John Luttrell. (Page 83)

HARRILL, JOHN
Administrator Account. 25 February, 1764. (Page 80)

GLASSCOCK, JOHN
8 March, 1765. 22 April, 1765.
Wife, Mary Glasscock, to have 1/2 of my estate whether "Riall or Persoal."
Daughter, Frances Glasscock, to have other 1/2 of estate.
Exrs: wife Mary and Thomas Glasscock to be my "hole and Soul" executors in this my last Will and Testament. (Page 87)

FRAZIER, DANIEL
28 May, 1765. 26 August, 1765.
Legatee: "To Samuel Anderson, Joiner, my chest that is at Reuben Berry's, and all that is in it, after funeral expenses are paid. Remainder of estate to Catherine Thatcher, if she is living, if deceased to Charles Haynes oldest son. Mary Bradford is to keep my mare until August next and then deliver to Catherine Thatcher.
Exrs: Charles Haynes.
Wit: Daniel Bradford, Joseph Morgan, Alexander Bradford. (Page 91)

PEARCE (PIERCE), PETER
6 February, 1768. 27 June, 1768.
To son, John, one slave.
Daughters, Rosannah and Susannah Pearce.
Wife, Lelia Pearce, to have land I purchased of William Waugh.
Exrs: brothers John and Jacob Pearce.
Wit: James Craig, Joseph Morgan, Elizabeth Maorgan. (Page 130)

LEES, MARY
29 October, 1767. Inventory.
Apprs: John Blackwell, Thomas Bronaugh, James Arnold.
(Page 131)

REYNOLDS, JOHN
21 Jan. 1769. Inventory.
Apprs: Thomas Marshall, John Keith, William Seaton.
(Page 141)

OWENS, JEREMIAH
26 Nov. 1772. 23 Oct. 1773.
Wife, Jane Owens.
Young son, Jeremiah Owens, to have slaves. Other children mentioned, but not named.
Wit: Evan Griffith, William Berry, John Owen, John Kenton.
(Page 261)

CHAMLAYNE, JAMES
26 Oct. 1775. Inventory.
Apprs: Joseph Blackerby, John Metcalfe, George Sullivan.
(Page 279)

(End of Book No. 1)

WILL BOOK NUMBER 2
1783 - 1796

FIELDING, EDWIN
11 January, 1781. 22 September, 1783
Wife, Nancy, to have 1/2 of Negroes, stock and household goods.
Sister, Elizabeth Reaves, to have other half of estate.
Exrs: wife and Joseph Taylor.
Wit: John James, Jeremiah Morgan, Henry Bradford, Elisabeth Bradford. (Page 4)

MOREHEAD, CHARLES
19 January, 1783. 27 October, 1783. Parish of Leeds.
Son, Turner Morehead, to have tract of land and 50 pounds of Virginia curr. Daughter, Jenny Ransdell, to have live stock.
Son, Charles Morehead, to have tract of land and household goods.
Daughter, Karenhappach Morehead, to have 80 pounds of Virginia curr.
Sons, Armistead, James, Pressley, to have land.
To daughter, Elizabeth Morehead, slaves, horse and saddle.
Wife, Mary Morehead, to have slaves during her life time.
To Ann Butler, for extraordinary service done, 5 pounds Virginia curr.
Exrs: wife, Charles Chilton, sons Turner and Charles Morehead.
(Page 6)

KELLY, JOHN
3 September, 1783
204 acres of land to be divided between Joseph Kelley and Joseph Henry, if Joseph Kelly does not return land to Joseph Henry's "eairs."
Wit: Edmond Holmes, Thomas Kelly, Mikel Glass. (Page 8)

JONES, JOHN
Inventory. 28 October, 1783.
Apprs: Peter Grant, John Ashby, John Shumate.
(Page 9)

BATTALEY, ANN
12 May, 1780. 24 Nov. 1783
To daughter, Hannah Battaley and son Fielding Battaley, all household goods, stock and all my part of my father's estate and 50 pounds that Col. Francis Tallaferrio left me in his will.
Exrs: dau. Hannah Battaley, Maxmillian Berryman, Battaley Bryan. (Page 10)

GARNER, DANIEL
Inventory. 24 Nov. 1783.
Apprs: Aaron Fletcher, James Withers, Benjamin Garner.
(Page 11)

WITHERS, JAMES
9 January, 1784. 26 January, 1784.
To son, George Washington Withers, (youngest son) 573 acres, slaves, furniture and gun.
To eldest son, James, a slave.
To daughter, Nancy Duncan, a slave.
To son, John, 1 slave.
To granddaughter, Betty McKay (dau. of Isaac & Betty), a slave.
Wife, Jemina.
Children: James, William, John, Hannah Pickett, Nancy Duncan, Betty Jennings. Exrs: Sons James and William, friend John Wigginton.
Wit: William Harris, Sabbatiah Isarel, John Wigginton. (Page 12)

DODD, NATHANIEL
9 May, 1783. 24 May 1784.
To daughter, Mildred Pinkard, slave.
To children of daughter Sarah Garner, 20 pounds of curr.
To son, Allen Dodd, a slave.
Daughter Hannah Hammit, to have 20 pounds of curr. Virginia money.
Daughter Elizabeth to receive 20 pounds. (Elizabeth Williamson)
To daughter, Mary Wheatley, 1 slave.
A slave to each of following named sons: John, Benjamin and James.
To wife, Sarah Dodd, part of estate during life.
Exrs: wife, sons James and Nathaniel.
Wit: Daniel Marr, Martha Allen, Paul Williams (Or Williamson)
(Page 24)

GLASSCOCK, JOHN
9 December, 1780. 28 June, 1784
Wife, mentioned, but not named.
Son Thomas to have 100 pounds of tobacco - he has received land.
To son, Hesekiah, a slave.
To son, George, a horse.
To daughter, Mary Rector, a pewter dish.
To daughter, Margaret Turley, furniture & bed.
Francis Jackson (son-in-law) to have what mr. William Brent owes me.
To son, John, 180 acres of land.
Exrs: wife and son John.
Wit: James Thompson, John Fishback, Philip Fishback. (Page 25)

EDMONDS, ELIAS
30 October, 1782. 28 June, 1784
All of estate to wife, Elizabeth Edmonds, at her decease to son Elias.
Daughters, Ann Hubbard, Judith Buckner, Elizabeth Bruin, to have all moveable estate now in their possession.
Exr: son Elias Edmonds.
Wit: Jacob Holtzclaw, John Hendley, William Jenkins, John ʳ -ker.
(Page 27)

MITCHELL, JOHN
26 June, 1784. Inventory.
Appr: James Crockett, Frederick Burnett, John Kemper. (Page 32)

CONWAY, THOMAS
25 August, 1784. 27 Sept. 1784.
To eldest son, William, slave.
To son, Thomas, a tract of land on Town Run.
To son, Peter, part of tract of land where I now live; remaining part to son Joseph.
To son, Henry, tract of land in Shenandoah County.
To daughter, Susannah Crosby, 5 pounds currency.
Grandson, James Conway (son of James), a slave.
Grandson, George Crosby, a slave.
To Sally Mausy, a slave.
Exrs: sons William, Thomas, Joseph.
Wit: Peter Grant, John Smith, Ann Smith.
(Page 39)

NEALE, JOSEPH
6 November, 1783. 24 May, 1784
To son, Benjamin, choice of a tract of land located by Squire Boon on the western waters and a rifle gun.
Wife, Mary, to have 1/3 of the estate, to be divided among daughters at her decease. Daughters: Sarah, Ann, Mary, Judah, Joanna and unborn child. Exrs: wife, Mathew Neale (brother) and Frederick Burdette.
Wit: Joseph Brugg, Frederick Burdette, John Burdette, William Suttle, John Bell. (Page 40)

NELSON, JOHN SR.
9 August, 1784. 25 October, 1784. Of Elk Run.
Sons, John and Jesse, to have tract of land in Shenandoah County.
Children: Jesse, John and William, Lida Morehead, Nanny Fishback, Mary Rector, Margaret Nelson, Jemina Nelson, Lettice Nelsen, Sarah Nelson. Exrs: wife, son William, friend Josias Fishback, Alexander Morehead. Wit: John Mathew, James Gillison, John Blackwell, Thomas Helm. (Page 46)

SHUMATE, JOHN
19 May, 1783. 25 October, 1784
Mentions son, Thomas Shumate.
To Capt. Jonathan Gibson, a tract of land.
To son, Bailey Shumate, 15 pounds of curr.
Sons, William, John, Joshua, Daniel, James and daughters, Lettice and Jemina, all property I gave them at the time of their marriage.
To wife, Judah Shumate, use of the estate.
Exrs: wife, Thomas Helm, John Nelson.
Wit: Thomas Helm, William Conway, John Kerr.
(Page 47)

BROWN, MARY
22 November, 1782. 27 October, 1784
Legatees: brothers and sisters: Elizabeth Priest, Marmaduke Brown, George Brown, Jonathan Brown, William Brown, Martin Brown, Frances Maddux, Sibby and Rebecca Brown. The three last mentioned shall have 50% less than the others. I give to sister Martha the deed of gift made to us by Sir Marmaduke Beckwith. To sister Elizabeth Priest, a saddle. To Peggy Brown, a silk bonnet.
Exrs: Marmaduke Brown, William Brown (bros.)
Wit: John Stark, Rodham Kenner, Peter Hodo. (Page 50)

ROBINSON, BENJAMIN
11 January, 1785. 28 February, 1785
Slaves are bequeathed to sons, Nathaniel, George, Dixon, Stephen, Elijah, James and John.
Daughters, Catherine Campbell, Elosha Robinson, Mary and Lydda Robinson, are bequeathed slaves.
To Ann Masters, 500 pounds of tobacco.
To wife (not named) slaves and land in Stafford County.
Exrs: sons Nathaniel, George and Dixon Robinson.
Wit: William White, William Nalle, Robert Gibson, Carr White. (Page 52)

NUGENT, ANN
23 May, 1785. 15 Sept. 1785.
To nephew, Lincefield Sharpe, slaves.
To brother, Edward Nugent, nephew William Ballard, niece Mary Ballard, 1000 pounds of tobacco and feather bed.
Wit: Peter Grant, Thomas Nugent, Susannah Grant. (Page 54)

KNOX, ROBERT
21 Sept. 1781. 29 August 1785. Charles County, Maryland.
Taken from county court of Charles County, Maryland.
To son, John Knox, land in Virginia (500 acres), slaves.
To son, Robert Dade Knox, all land in Maryland.
To daughter, Janet Knox, land in Virginia, slaves.
As no provision has been made for unborn child -- to have 800 pounds sterling. To wife, Rose Townsend, to have whatever it is customary to give widow in the part of the world where my estate lyes"
Exrs: wife Rose Townsend, Col. Robert Hooe (of Alexandria), Andrew Bailee, Alexander B. Martin.
Wct: G.R. Brown, Verlinda Martin, Andrew Bailee, Will Millar.
(Page 57)

THORNHILL, BRYANT
13 October, 1785. 21 October, 1785.
Son, Charles Thornhill, to have property that came from his mother.
Daughters: Elizabeth and Parthenia.
(Con. on page 40)

Sons, James, William and Elijah.
Wife, Leannah Thornhill.
Exrs: William Hunton, Robert Sanders.
Wit: James Lawler, James Hunton.
(Page 75)

PEARL, WILLIAM
24 May, 1785. 28 July 1785
Grandson, William Fearle (son of Samuel) to have tract of land after decease of grandmother, Martha Pearl.
Land to daughter, Elizabeth, during her life, at her decease to her son, Elijah. To daughter, Margaret Fields (wife of John), 100 acres of land.
Slaves to daughters, Sarah Smares, Martha Evins, Mary Murray.
To grandchildren: William, John, Elizabeth and Anne Weadon, 10 pounds each. To son, Samuel, 50 pounds curr. should he die to his son William.
To son, William, 1000 pounds of tobacco. Son Richard ----
To wife, all estate during widowhood-- children to receive bequest after her decease. Daughter, Elizabeth Cundiffe alias Ellitt.
Exrs: wife, Samuel Fearle, Ralph Murry.
Wit: Reuben Strother, Daniel Brown, Benjamin Carpenter, Reuben Elliott, Benjamin Strother.   (Page 61)

NEALE, BEN
23 March, 1779. 26 April, 1785. Parish of Leeds.
"All Wareing Cloathes to be divided equally between two sons, Jesse and Moses, but if one dies then all to the longest liver."
All rest of estate to beloved wife (not named).
Exr: wife.
Wit: Rebecca Hich, Christopher Hich, Clement Norma.
(Page 76)

SMITH, JOSEPH
Account. 24 Oct. 1785. .(Page 77).

PARKER, ALEXANDER
9 May, 1785. 28 Nov. 1785.
To wife, Amy Parker, slaves and land at her decease to sons Richard and William Parker. Children: Richard, William. Elizabeth Scott and Lucy Parker.
If unborn child be a son, name is to be Alexander, if a girl to be named Judy.
Exrs: wife and brother Richard.
Wit: Benjamin Neale, Catesby Woodford, Rawley Hogain.
(Page 78)

LAURENCE, EDWARD
26 March, 1763. 27 March, 1786.
(Con. on page 41)

To son, John Laurence, slaves.
To son, Peter, 5 slaves. Son, Edward, to have 6 slaves.
Daughter, Susannah Catlett, to have 5 shillings.
Daughters, Sarah Priest, Winnifred Luttrell, Joan Wicks, to have slaves.
Grandson, Rodham Tulles Laurence, 2 slaves & feather bed.
To son, Richard, land and plantation where I now live (377 acres and 14 slaves.
Exr: son Richard Laurence.
Wit: Original Young, Thomas Conway, Richard Priest, William Crosby.
(Page 82).

MARTIN, CHARLES
12 January, 1785: 27 March, 1786.
All estate to daughters, Catherine Baylie and Susan Allen.
Daughters, Elisabeth Edwards, Mary Pore, Frances Wade and -- McCarty, to receive 1 shilling each.
Exrs: Catherine Baylie, Susan Allen.
Wit: William Carter, Joseph Bailey, Samuel Haslerig, Margaret Mason.
(Page 84)

MCCORMICK, STEPHEN
3 February, 1786. 26 June, 1786. Of Hamilton Parish.
Wife, Margaret McCormick, to have use of estate, at her decease it is to be divided between son John McCormick and daughter, Elizabeth Mountjoy Martin. To daughter, Ann Shumate, cow and calf.
Exrs: wife, son and Gavin Lawson.
Wit: Paul Williams, James Haydon, William Jones.
(Page 89)

RAMSDELL, WHARTON
27 January, 1786. 26 June, 1786.
1000 Acres to be sold and money divided among the following named children: William Ramsdell, Anne Morehead, Margaret Ramsdell, Sarah Ramsdell. Twenty pounds to be reserved for the education of grandsons, Charles Morehead Ramsdell and Wharton Ramsdell, also to have a tract of land in Jefferson County. To son-in-law, Cadwallor Slaughter, 2 slaves. To daughter, Ann Morehead, 5 slaves; dau. Margaret, 5 slaves; dau. Sarah, 4 slaves. Slaves bequeathed to sons, Edward, John and William. Son Thomas to have slaves and wearing apparel. Son Wharton Ramsdell, Jr. deceased.
Exrs: Charles Chilton, Elias Edmonds, Thomas Ramsdell, Sr., William Ramsdell, Jr., Thomas Ramsdell, Sr. (Page 93)

SCOTT, JOHN
9 February, 1783. 27 April, 1785. Dettengen Parish, Prince William County. Estate to be divided between all children in America and Great Britain.
Wife, Elizabeth, to have 1/2 of estate during widowhood.
Mentions "Aunt Elizabeth Innes, of Great Britain." (Con. page 42)

Exrs: wife, (should she remarry son Robert to take her place),
friend Thomas Blackburn, William Alexander, Esquire.
Wit: Cuthbert Bullitt, Alexander Scott, Thomas Fitzhugh.
(Page 99)

HATHAWAY, JOHN
13 April, 1786. 25 April, 1786
To wife, Sarah Hathaway, land and slaves, after her decease estate
to be divided between children, Judy Kamper, Sarah Bartlett, Elizabeth
Hathaway, John, Nancy, Susannah, Molly, Dolly, Peggy Lawson, Sarepta,
Francis. Daughters, Juday and Sarah to have 2 pounds less than the
others. Son, John Hathaway, to have land which Simon Kenton was to
locate for me.
Exrs: wife and son John.
Wit: Josiah Fishback, Philip Fishback.
(Page 104)

DARNALL, DAVID
22 March, 1785. 23 October, 1786.
To wife, Mary, all estate during her life.
Son, John.
Granddaughter, Molly Lees (or Leer).
Grandson, John Shaver.
Exrs: wife and son John.
Wit: Eave Riley, Edward Riley, William Pickett.
(Page 111)

WILLIAMS, GEORGE
13 November, 1786. 25 December, 1786.
Wife, Ann Williams, to have 1/2 of plantation during her life time.
To son, Elijah, 1/2 of plantation.
Grandsons: Richardson and George Williams (sons of John).
To daughter, Elizabeth Butler, all estate she has received and 25
shillings. To grandson, Benjamin Butler, if living, 7 pounds, if
not to surviving brother. Grandson, John Butler (son of John), 7
pounds curr. Daughter, Catherine Williams, to be supported during
life. Sons, William, George, Elijah.
Daughter, Margaret Freeman. Grandchildren: James, George and
Ann Collins, children of dau. Ann Collins, dec'd.
Exrs: sons George and William.
Wit: James Routt, Augustine Jennings, Joseph Selman. (Page 112)

BLACKWELL, JOSEPH
26 April, 1787. 25 June, 1787
Wife to have use of estate during life.
Sons, Joseph, Samuel, John and George Steptoe.
Daughter, Judith Keith.
Son-in-law, Martin Pickett.   Daughters: Ann, Lucy, Betty, Judah.
Exrs: wife and four sons.   (Con. page 43)

Wit: Peter Grant, Peter Conway, James Thompson.
(Page 116)

KEITH, ISHAM
13 March, 1787. 24 Sept. 1787
To wife, Charlotte Keith, 1/3 of estate during life.
Son, John, to have all land in Fauquier County and land allowed me
as a Continental officer.   Daughters, Betty, Mary Isham Keith,
Sarah Ashmore, Caty Gallashue Keith, Charlotte Ashmore Keith.
Exrs: wife, brother Thomas Keith, Charles Martin.
Wit: William Hunton, William White, George Roach.
(Page 119)

HEALEY, JOHN
2 April, 1787. 22 October, 1787.
Wife, Mary Healey, to have use of estate as long as she remains a
widow, after that only what the law allows her.
Exrs: John Dareing, John Morehead (friends).
Wit: James Genn, Celie Genn, James Ball.
(Page 122)

CHINN, CHARLES
13 May, 1787. 25 February, 1788.
To son, Charles, silver watch, household goods.
Sons: Rawleigh, John, William Ball, Nancy Chinn, to have household
goods. Son Elijah to have 500 acres of land in County of Nelson,
District of Kentucky. All residue of land in Kentucky to be divided
between sons, Charles, John, Rawleigh, William and Joseph Chinn.
Wife, Seth Chinn, to have land in Loudon and Fauquier Counties.
Daughter, Lila Reno. Daughters, Penelope, Betty, Margaret, Betty
and Sukey. Son, Christopher Chinn.
Sons, Charles, Raleigh and John and friend Rawleigh Chinn, Sr. are
named as executors.
Wit: John French, Daniel French, Ralph Murry. (Page 125)

SETTLES, GAYTON
9 July, 1787. 25 February, 1788.
Wife Mary to have whole estate during life and at her decease it is
to go to son William. Exrs: wife and son.
Wit: John Askins, Edward Settles. (Page 127)

MOXIE, THOMAS
19 May, 1786. 28 April, 1788.
Mrs. Elizabeth Scott, widow of my friend, James Scott, Esq., to be
paid the annuity left me by my friend, Rev. Mr. James Scott, from
death of his widow, Sarah Scott, dec'd. until my death, also rest of
my estate. Exrs: Mrs. Elizabeth Scott.
Wit: Charles Chilton, William Stewart.   (Page 183)

HAMILTON, WILLIAM
17 August, 1784. 23 June, 1786.
To brother, Henry Hamilton, all slaves and land.
To sister, Rebecca Thrift, 10 pounds of currency; to her son, Hamilton, a watch. Legatees: William Waddle, Thomas Skinner, Thomas Keith, John Ridley.
Exrs: Thomas Keith, Isham Keith.
Wit: John Ridley, William Waddell. (Page 133)

WADDELLS, JOHN
1 April, 1788. 23 June, 1788
Estate to be divided between Mathew Waddell and all my children at decease of wife Elizabeth.
To daughter, Teny Murphy, 1 shilling.
Children: William, James, George, Margaret, Elizabeth, Polly, John, Frances. Exrs: wife and son William.
Wit: Joseph Taylor, John Coppadge, James May. (Page 134)

BLAND, THOMAS
1 April, 1788. 22 Sept. 1788.
To son, Thomas, all land in Prince William County.
To son, James (youngest), land in Prince William County.
Daughters, Catherine and Mary Bland.
Exrs: wife, Jane Bland, Thomas Bland, Benjamin Harrison.
Wit: John Lansdown. (Page 136)

BARKER, WILLIAM
27 May, 1788. 27 October, 1788. Of Parish of Leeds.
Wife, Susannah Barker, to have estate as long as she remains a widow. Children: Charles, Nanny, Mary Parker, James and William. Children who are married have been provided for.
Exrs: William Barker (son), Richard Parker.
Wit: Hugh Bradley, Matt. Waddell, Jeremiah Morgan. (Page 138)

GRIGSBY, WILLIAM
29 December, 1788. 25 June, 1789.
Daughters: Fanny Rout, Winnifred, Eady.
Granddaughter, Jane Rout.
Sons, Lewis, Bayliss, Nathaniel, to have slaves.
Exrs: son Lewis and Richard Rout.
Wit: Hezekiah Turner, John White, John Catlett. (Page 146)

RECTORS, HARMON
23 Sept. 1792. 28 Sept. 1789
To son, Harmon, 100 acres lying in the German Town and slaves.
Household goods to be divided between three sons.
Exrs: Capt. Tillman Weaver, John Martin.
Wit: Charles Utterback, Henry Utterback, William Nelson. (Page 147)

CRUMP, JOHN
5 February, 1789. 23 September, 1789
To son, George Crump, 5 shillings.
Daghters, Elizabeth Utterback, Mary Waugh, Hannah Branan, Ann Lewis, to
have 5 shillings each. Daughters, Sarah and Catherine to have feather
beds. Son, John, to have all land where I now live unless "he takes up
and marries a certain woman by name of Mary Westall." Land to go to son
Daniel if son John marries Mary Westall.
Exrs: brothers George and Benjamin Crump, William Eustace, Jr., John
James. Wit: John James, John Shumate, Mason Shumate. (Page 148)

Allotment of Dower of Jemina Harris, late widow of James Withers, dec'd.
27 July, 1789.

HALEY, HONOR
27 February, 1787. 25 January, 1790
To son, Michael Cavanaugh, all money.
Legatees: Mary Johnston (dau. of Henry Peyton), Sarah Fishback (dau. of
Josias Fishback), 1 guinea, John Morcy, 5 pounds curr.
Exrs: Josias Fishback, Henry Peyton.
Wit: George Leach, Sr., George Leach, Jr., James Fishback. (Page 153)

EBRY, ROBERT
Sons, Thomas and Robert to receive land.
Grandson, Robert Embrey (son of Charles, dec'd.)
Exrs: sons Thomas and Robert
Wit: Susannah Brown, John Brown. (Page 157)
26 Oct. 1784. 25 Jan. 1790.

BUTTON, HARMON
25 December, 1789. 25 January, 1790.
Lends to wife, Catherine, during her life.
Son, Jacob Button, dau. Ann Hockman, Sarah Sinsee to have land that is
now in their possession.
Daughters: Susan, Rebecca and Catherine Button.
Exrs: John Kemper, Sr. and Jacob Kemper, Sr.
Wit: Charles Kemper, Robert Turnbull, Rand Smith. (Page 158)

NUGENT, THOMAS
11 Sept. 1789. 22 Feb. 1790.
To nephew, Lincefield Sharpe, all land where I now live, slaves, cattle.
Mentions children of brother Edward Nugent.
Nephew Thomas Nugent to receive slaves.
Brother, Edward Nugent, title to a tract of land.
To niece, Mary Hampton's two daughters, Frances and Susannah.
To Ann Nugent Sharpe (dau. of Lincefield Sharpe).
Nephew, William Ballard.
Exr: brother Edward Nugent. (Page 160)

GARNER, BENJAMIN
5 Sept. 1789. 26 April, 1790
Wife, Diannah Garner.
Children mentioned, but not named.
Exrs: wife, Vincent Garner (bro.), James Withers.
Wit: James Withers, John Withers, James Garner. (Page 166)

EMBREY, ANN
9 February, 1790. April, 1790. Nuncupative will.
To son, Robert Embrey, household goods, stock.
To daughter, Elizabeth Taylor.
Son, John Embrey.
To daughter, Nancy Butler, my saddle.
This will was proved by the oaths of William Snelling, Alexander Brown, Sarah Benjey. (Page 167)

THROCKMORTON, FRANCES
2 May, 1790. 27 Sept. 1790.
Legatees: brother William Throckmorton, sisters Mary and Ann Throckmorton. Exrs: Morgan Tomkils (friend) of Glouchester County.
Wit: H. Brooks, Frances Brooks. (Page 174)

SANDERS, ROBERT
27 May, 1790. 22 Sept. 1790
To son, William a tract of land.
Sons, James, Brittain, Gabriel, Thomas, Lewis, Larking Sanders.
Exrs: James Sanders, William Hunton, James Hunton, Thomas Sanders.
Wit: Charles Chilton, William Hunton, Jr., Elizabeth Sanders.
(Page 175)

LEE, RICHARD
24 Sept. 1790. 25 Oct. 1790
To sister, Priscilla, 200 pounds currency:
To brother, Arthur, horse and bridle.
Brothers: William, George, Kendall, Hancock and Arthur.
Sisters, Betty Edwards, Judith Pierce.
Exrs: brother George Lee, Thomas Edwards.

BURGESS, GARNER
19 April, 1790. October, 1790
Wife: Anne Burgess.
Children: Susannah, James, Peggy, John, Nancy, Mary Neal, Sarah Settle, Edward and John Burgess.
Exrs: wife, son Edward, Matthew Neal.
Wit: B. Shackleford, Matthew Neal, Isaac Arnold.
(180)

BROWNING, CALEB
Inventory. 14 Dec. 1787. July 1791. (Page 201)

WITHERS, JAMES
4 May, 1791.   July 1791.
Children: Thomas, John, Elisabeth, Hannah, Cain, Lucy, Centy, Enoch, William, Sithey, Sally and Patty.
Exrs: wife Elizabeth and son John. (Page 202)

GIBSON, JONATHAN
22 July, 1788. 26 Sept. 1791
Three youngest children: Joanathan Catlett, Susanna Grayson, Mary.
Slaves bequeathed to sons, Thomas, John, Jonathan Catlett Gibson.
To daughters, Ann Grayson Blackwell, Susanna Gibson and Mary Gibson, to have slaves. Granddaughter, Margaret Catlett Gibson and children of dau. Ann G. Blackwell, to have slaves, also niece Mary Adie, to have slave.
Exrs: sons Thomas, John, Jonathan and Benjamin Harrison.
Wit: John Mausy, Mathew Harrison, Jr.   (Page 204)

NELSON, JOHN
22 March, 1791. December, 1791
Wife, Mary, to have use of estate during life.
Land to be divided between the following legatees, two daughters of James Nelson, dec'd., Elizabeth Green and Catherine Horton.
1/5 part to Hannah James, wife of Thomas James.
1/5 part to Mary Nelson, widow of John Nelson, Jr. dec'd.
1/5 part to Thomas Nelso (son).
1/5 part to Joseph Nelson (son).
Exrs: wife, William Phillips (of Stafford Co.), Garrett Gray, Jr.
Wit: Original Young, John Green, Elizabeth James. (Page 210)

YOUNG, WILLIAM
20 December, 1790. February, 1792
Wife, Patience Young, to have use of estate during her life.
To son, William, slave.
To daughter, Mary Jeffries, slave.
To daughters, Hannah Orsley (or Crosley), Sukey (Susannah Smith) 20 pounds of curr.
Exrs: Joseph Jeffries, Thomas Fitzhugh.
Wit: Menoah Stone, Edward Fegan, Benjamin Carpenter. (Page 214)

ASHBY, ROBERT
2 June, 1790. 27 February, 1792
Son, Benjamin, to have a tract of land on Shenandoah River, where he now lives, and slaves.
Grandson, William Ashby (son of Benjamin) to have slaves.
Lends to son Enoch and wife Sally, a tract of land, after the decease of Enoch land to go to sons of Enoch, Robert and Alexander.
Daughter Ann Farrow, 10 pounds curr. (Con. on page 48)

To grandson, Bayliss Ashford, 1 feather bed.
To gr. daughter, Molly Farguson, 1 feather bed.
To daughter, Winnifred Peper, 1 cow - no more.
Grandsons, Martin and Thomas Ashby (son of Nimrod), 1 slave.
To daughter, Molly Athel, 1 gown - no more.
Grandson, Benjamin Farrow, 1 slave.
Exr: son John.
Wit: William Withers, John Clark, John Fishback. (Page 216)

WRIGHT, JOHN
1 June, 1785. 7 February, 1792
To son James, land and slaves.
To granddaughter, Betsy Wright (dau. of James Wright), slaves.
Daughters, Mary and Rosamond, to have plantation where I now live.
Wife, Elizabeth Wright.
Sons, William and John Wright, to have 20 shilling each - the land I gave them they sold.
Should Elizabeth Parlow ever apply to be given 15 pounds curr.
Exrs: daughters, Mary and Rosamond.
Wit: George Maddox, John Nelson, Francis Lathane. (Page 219)

COCKRELL, ANDERSON
7 Sept. 1791. 27 Sept. 1792
Daughter, Rosanna Cockrell, 1 mare
Son, William, to have a horse.
Estate to be kept together until youngest daughter, Sally Cockrell, arrives at the age of 18 years.
Exrs: brother Jesse Moffett and son William.
Wit: John Cooke, John Porter, Augustine Bannister. (Page 221)

FREEMAN, JAMES
Youngest daughter, Sally, to have feather bed and household furniture with full benefits and profits of part of her grandfather, George Williams, estate, which was bequeathed to her mother - this to descend at mother's death.
Wife, Margaret Freeman, to have 1/3 of estate during life.
Grandson, Gollop Freeman (alias Duncan), household goods.
Sons, Garrett and Nathaniel, personal estate and slaves.
Daughter, Mary Hackley (wife of James) to have 30 shillings - she has received her share. Daughter, Elinor Silman (wife of Joseph), 1 pounds curr. Sons: William, James, Garrett, Nathaniel Freeman.
Daughter, Elizabeth Fletcher (wife of John), to have money from sale of land. Exrs: wife, sons William and James.
Wit: Samuel Wharton, Jr., William Williams, James Routt. (Page 226)

TOLLE, STEPHEN
9 Oct. 1791. 25 June 1792. Nuncupative will.
Wife Anne to have whole estate until son George comes of age. Mentions unborn child. Appoints George Tolle and Enoch Crosby to conduct affairs for wife. Wit: Samuel Pearle, George Tolle, Francis Murray. (Page 231)

WOODFORD, CATESBY
8 Sept. 1791. 24 Sept. 24 Sept. 1792
Lends to wife, Mary, all of estate.
Desires that sons be educated according to value of estate.
Exrs: wife, son Mark (when he comes of age), friends George Buckner, Jr. and William Woodford.
Wit: Thomas Montgomerie, Y. Johnson. (Page 242)

ROGER, GEORGE
Wife, Betty Roger, to have use of estate.
Sons: George and Edward.
Daughters, Betty Newby and Mary Sanders.
1/5 part of estate to be used in support of daughter, Sally Mathew, and children. Mentions "trusty friend" Ambrose Barnett.
Exrs: sons George and Edward.
Wit: Samuel Steele, Henry Steele, Robert Gibson.
4 May, 1792. 24 Sept. 1792 (Page 244)

TAYLOR, HENRY
Inventory. 6 Sept. 1792

BULLITT, JOSEPH
17 November, 1792. 24 December, 1792.
Daughter, Susan Redd to have 5 slaves and her sons, Joseph Bullitt Redd and Formorcis Redd, to have a slave each.
Daughter, Mary Steatard to have 4 slaves, her son, Joseph Steatard to have 1 slave. Joseph Bullitt Rodd, son of Priscilla, to have 3 slaves.
Wife, Barsheba Norman, now Bullitt, use of 3 slaves, furniture and land.
Exrs: Thomas Conway, Original Young, John Young.
Wit: Peter Conway, Charles Coppadge, William Young. (Page 249)

KENNER, RODHAM
5 June, 1793. 28 June, 1793
Daughters, Lucy and Judith Kenner, to have 200 acres of land when they become of age. Son Lawerence to have rest of land and slaves.
Son, Lawerence, to be given to his uncle, Rodham Kenner, if he is inclined to take him, when 10 years of age. Desire that he be placed in a seminary where he may be well ingrafted with the French language only.
Exrs: Rodham Kenner, Samuel Blackwell, Judith Kenner.
Wit: Samuel Blackwell, James Seaton, Jonathan Brown. (Page 252)

HEADLEY, JAMES
11 Dec. 1792. 28 June, 1793
Wife, Lucy, to have all of estate during life or widowhood.
Father and mother mentioned, but not named, also children.
Exrs: Eppa Timberlake, William Day, John Cooke.
Wit: John Cooke, James Ready, William Day.
(Page 254)

MORGAN, SIMON
10 November, 1792. 25 February, 1793
Son, Joseph, to have 162 acres of land which I now liveon, part of a
tract of 486 acres. Son Charles to receive a tract of land.
Son, Simon, tract of land. Son, Jeremiah, personal preperty.
To daughter, Sukey Clark, cow & calf.
Daughter, Caty Bradford.
Daughter, Rosey Cockrin (wife of William), to have 1 shilling.
Exrs: sons Simon and Joseph.
Wit: Hugh Bradley, George Carter, William Carter.
(Mention is made of late wife.)   (Page 260)

SMITH, JOSEPH
6 January, 1793. February, 1793. Of Parish of Leeds.
Son William to have 200 acres of land, tract on which I now live.
Daughters, Mary Burdette, Hannah Ball, to have slaves.
To son, John, slaves, wearing apparel, 1 chest that was my fathers.
To sons, Rowley and Enoch, slaves.
Daughter, Lucy Popper, to have slaves.
Grandson, Abner Smith, slaves, granson to be taken care of by son, John
Smith. To sister, Jean Owing, 10 pounds currency.
Granddaughters: Ruth Smith and Willamina.
Daughter, Joan Porter.
Exrs: Sons, Rowley, John and John Porter.
Wit: William Dulin, David Ball, Benjamin Ball, William Redding.
(Page 263)

MANUEL, FRANCIS
6 September, 1792. November, 1793.
Daughter, Abbe Manuel, to have all stock and furniture.
Exrs: Daughter Abbe Manuel and her son, Zachariah Manuel.
(Page 266)

JOHNSON, SMITH
Inventory. February 16, 1793.
Apprs: John Dearing, Joseph Smith, John Morehead, Sr.   (Page 270)

WEST, IGNATUS
16 Sept. 1791. 22 July, 1793. Of Spottsylvania Co.
Daughter, Mary Haner, to have 17 pounds and 2 shillings, placed in the
hands of Mr. Harmon Haner (her father-in-law).
Daughter, Elisabeth Bolling.
Other children mentioned, but not named.
Exr: son Benjamin West.   (Page 280)

MARTIN, JOSEPH, SR.
4 November, 1791. 1793.
(Con. on page 51)

Youngest son, Benjamin Martin.
Eldest son, John Martin, heirs of son Enoch, dec'd., all my sons and daughters to have equal share of estate.
Exrs: wife, Katherine Martin, Charles Martin.
Wit: John Fletcher.
(Under the signature of Joseph Martin is written Hosea Martin) (Page 281)

FLETCHER, THOMAS
3 November, 1792. 22 July, 1793.
Son, John, to care for mother, brother and sisters.
Exrs: Richard Fletcher, John Fletcher, Thomas Fletcher.
Wit: John Dawson, Thomas Ball, Richard Fisher, William Pinchard.
(Page 283)

DUNCAN, JOSEPH
13 February, 1792. 23 Sept. 1793
Wife, Lydia, to have use of land and slaves during life.
Children: Joseph, Hyma Mausy, Rose Withers, Hannah Porter, Houser Duncan, Mary Wright, Lydia Obannon.
Exrs: Joseph and Houser (sons), John Obannon (son-in-law) and John Mauzy (son-in-law).
Wit: John Kerr, Peter Kemper, James Parr. (Page 284)

GLASCOCK, JAMES
1 July, 1793. 23 September, 1793
Wife, Agatha to hold estate during her life, "without making any waste."
Wit: Charles Dulaney, Lucy Fishback, Elizabeth Cunningham.

ALLEN, URSULLA
12 August, 1789. ---1793
My father, James Withers, of Stafford County, bequeathed to me 2 slaves—my late husband left those slaves by will and testament to his sons, William, James, Joseph Allen and his dau. Ann Bradford, to be given them at my decease, and doubt has arisen as to whether said husband had right to dispose of said Negroes.
To daughter, Ann Bradford, all my wearing apparel.
Grandsons: Baldwin Bradford and Armistead Minor.
Sons, Thomas, Joseph, James Allen.
Money to be paid widows of sons, John and William Allen.
Exrs: Sons Thomas, James and Joseph Allen.

HURST, ROSANNA
17 October, 1793. 28 Oct. 1793
Son, Henry Hurst.
One shilling each to following named daughters: Elizabeth Thompson (wife of Jesse), Mildred Markwell (wife of William), Nancy Hoffering (wife of Augustin), Dolly Crum (wife of Joseph). Daughter Jane Hurst, to have personal property.
Wit: John Ferguson, Gracey Quisenberry, Sally Thompson. (Page 303)

DUNCAN, JOHN
4 April, 1788. 23 December, 1795
To son, John, to have 10 shillings. Son-in-law, Benjamin Grigsby, 5 shillings. All estate to be sold when son, Willis Duncan, "arrives to the age 20 years." Wife, Wilky Duncan. Children: Moses, Enoch, Willis, Milly, Lucinda.
Exrs: Charles Duncan, Moses Duncan (sons)
(Page 312)   Wit: Charles Duncan, Cossom Day, Margaret Williams.

RILEY, JOHN
21 January, 1791. 23 December, 1791
Sons: Thomas, Hugh, Edward, John, George and Charles.
To daughter, Catherine Darnall, 10 pounds curr. money.
Daughters: Elizabeth Gear, Lettice Fenner, Mary Hill.
Grandson, Charles Riley and gr.dau. Catherine Riley (father Charles Riley), Susan Riley (dau. of Edward Riley).
Exrs: Edward, Thomas and Hugh Riley (sons).
Wit: William Pickett, Francis Triplett, Reuben Bramlett, John Riley (son of Thomas).

MORGAN, SIMON
Inventory. 24 June, 1794
(Page 323)

BALL, JAMES
20 February, 1794. September, 1794
Wife, Nancy, to have estate during life.
Children: Peggy Stevinson, Judy Ball, Lucy Ball, Shealtial Ball, Talliaferrie Ball, Elizabeth Ball, James Ball, John Ball, Nancy Ball and unborn child.
Exrs: Benjamin Stephinson, John Singleton.
(Page 328)

BARKER, JOHN
25 September, 1794. 24 October, 1794
Three oldest children, Elizabeth, Mary and Chloe, to have slaves when Chloe is eighteen. Other daughters, Ann, Milly and Sarah.
Wife, Sarah Barker.
Exrs: John Glasscock, George Adams.
Wit: John Monroe, John Rawlins.   (Page 332)

LYNN, JOHN
18 August, 1794. December, 1794.
Sons, John and Lewis, to have tract of land where I now live.
Son, Francis, to have 20 pounds curr., has received his share of estate.
Children: Fielding, Thompson, Sukey Thomas, Gr.dau. Jane West.
Exrs: sons Fielding and Thompson, Lewis Lynn.
Wit: Charles Metcalf, James Lawson, Thomas Lawson. (Page 345)

WAITE, JANE
1 April, 1794. 22 December, 1794
Legatees: Mr. Richard Eustace Beale, Willy Roy and William Bronaugh (brother). Slaves to be liberated.
Slaves, Bob and Lucy, to have 20 acres of land.
Mrs. Margaret Beale to have my shag cream case, with 6 spoons, tongs and strainer.
Exr: Capt. Thomas Gibson.
Wit: John Fox, William Eustace, Jr., Lyons Luckett. (Page 346)

TRIPLETT, FRANCIS
24 September, 1794. January, 1795
Children: William, Hedgman, Robert, Betty, Benedicte, Anne and Frances.
Amelia Triplett to have 20,000 acres of land on the north fork of Licking.
Son, Robert, to have land in Kentucky.
Daughters, Betty and Benedicte, to have a tract of land in Kentucky, County of Bourbon, containing 1400 acres.
To wife, Benedicte, and daughters, Ann and Frances (youngest) to have 5000 acres of land in Kentucky, upon Cabin Creek. Moveable estate to be sold and money used to defray expenses to Kentucky.
Exrs: sons William and Robert Triplett. (Page 347)

WITHERS, THOMAS
5 November, 1794. December, 1795.
Sons: John, Enoch, Mathew Keen, Joseph, William and Benjamin.
Daughters: Hannah Winn, Betty Winn, Nancy Jordan, Sally West, Susan Chinn. Granddaughter, Hannah Winn (dau. of Betty Winn), legacy to be in care of her father, Capt. Minor Winn.
Mention is made that he is at law with brother, William Winn, about land. Also that he is trying to recover money from Isaac Hite (or Hitt), administrator of James Buchanan, dec'd.
Exrs: sons William and Capt. Minor Winn.
(Page 349)

ROGERS, JOHN
8 August, 1794. 22 December, 1794
Son, Henry and wife Sarah and their youngest son, John.
Children: Stephen, John, Mary Rogers and Mary Mason.
Exr: son Henry
Wit: Daniel Greenwood, James Dennis, Mathew Neal. (Page 354)

OLDAKER, ABRAHAM
10 December, 1794. 27 April 1795
Wife, Hester, to have use of estate during her life.
Mention is made of 8 children, but they are not named.
Exr: wife
Wit: Joseph Sheetsa, Benjamin Sheetzs, Benjamin Taylor.
(Page 560)

MCKENNEY, JOHN
24 January, 1795.   22 June 1795
Son, John, to have 200 acres of land, cattle, sheep, household goods.
To son, Francis, 1 shilling.
Wife, Mary, 1 shilling.
Daughters: Mary Cain, Elizabeth McKenney, Alice McKenney, to have 1
shilling each.   Granddaughter, Susannah McKenney (dau. of John), to have
1 slave.
Exr: son John
Wit: Nimrod Otterback, Ezekial Davis, David Evan, Daniel Carter.
(Page 366)

SUDDUTH, WILLIAM
10 November, 1785.   June, 1795
Lends to wife, Alse, estate during her life, at her decease to be divided
among all my children. (not named)
Mentions daughter, Mary Sudduth.
Exrs: sons Francis and George Sudduth.
Wit: Edward Settle, Benjamin Arnold, John Forrester.
(Page 367)

DARNALL, JEREMIAH
10 April, 1795.   June, 1795
Wife, Catherine Darnall
Children: Elizabeth Sinclair, Joseph, Ann Weaver, Mary Russell (to have
500 acres in Kentucky), Margaret Sinclair, Susannah Smith (20 shillings),
Leannah Ashby, Caty Darnall, Rosamond Darnall. Granddaughter, Lucy Ashby.
Exr: James Wright (friend)
Wit: William Weaver, John Martin, Henry Kearns.
(Page 368)

PRIEST, THOMAS
15 February, 1790.   28 Sept. 1795
Wife, Sarah, to have use of estate during her life time.
Children: Peter and Mary Priest, other children mentioned, but not named.
Exrs: wife and son Thomas.
Wit: Richard Larrance, William Coppedge, Edward Larrance. (Page 378)

KIDWELL, MARY
16 March, 1795.   Sept. 1795
Son, William Kidwell.
George Thompson, Joshua Drummond and Nathaniel Snope (sons-in-law) to have
remainder of estate.
Exrs: Henry Peyton, Sr. and Henry Peyton, Jr. (Page 379)

BROOKS, THOMAS
20 January, 1792.   October, 1795.
Wife, Elizabeth, to have land during her widowhood. (Con. on page 55)

Sons: Thomas, William and John.
Daughters, Elizabeth Brown, Nancy Fox, Sally Brown, Winny Northcutt, Mary and Dorcas Brooks. (Page 381)

BARBEE, ANDREW
28 December, 1790. 28 Dec. 1795
Wife, Jane Barbee, to have land and slaves during life.
Sons: Andrew and John.
Daughters: Elizabeth, Mary Poley, Sarah Bradford.
Grandsons: Abijah Withers, son of dau. Elizabeth Withers; Thomas and Andrew Russell Barbee (sons of Joseph).
Exrs: sons Andrew and John Barbee.
Wit: B. Shackleford, Thomas Harris, Aquilla Divis.
(Page 387)

BELL, FRANCES
14 December, 1796. 28 December, 1795.
All estate to grandson, William Bell.
Exrs: Elias Edmonds, William Edmonds, Jr., Eppa Timberlake (friends).
Wit: John Edmonds, James Edmonds, Sarah Timberlake.
(Page 389)

PETERS, JOHN
Inventory. October 1781-1784

(End of Book No.2)

WILL BOOK NUMBER 3

1796--1803

GRIFFITH, EVAN
10 Sept. 1795. 25 April, 1796
To son, John, wearing apparel
Son, Willoughby to have land. Son Dennis to have plantation after decease of mother.
Daughters, Amelia Owens, Rachel Creel, Peggy Griffith and Susannah Griffith, to have land in Kentucky.
Wfe, Sarah, to have land during widowhood.
Daughter, Sarianne, to have land and personal property.
Exrs: wife and son Elijah.
Wit: Benjamin Goldsmith, Rachel Flynn, William Flynn.

BROWN, MOLLY
28 February, 1796. 2 March, 1796.
Legatees: George Brooke and heirs,(George, Francis, Mathew and Anne Brooks); Kitty Powell, Elizabeth Diggs, Lucy Brooke, furniture and books.
Will was proven by the oath of William Chilton that Molly Brown, wife of Robert Brown Gentleman, made the above nuncupative will in the house of Thomas Digges and that she died sometime that night.
(Page 3)

Division of property between Mary Brown, widow of William Seaton, dec'd. and his two sons, James and William Seaton. Mention is made of David Wickliffe as an heir. Oct. 2, 1795
(Page 6)

GARNER, VINCENT
28 August, 1795. 27 June, 1796.
Son, John, land adjoining James Withers line - formerly purchased of Jonas Garner.
To son, Jonas, what land is now in his possession and 10 shillings.
To heirs of daughter, Sarah Suttle (hus. William).
Gr.son James Withers.
Wife, Jemima to have land during widowhood.
Children: Vincent, William, Jesse, Elizabeth, Jemima Harris (hus; William). Wit: Enoch Withers, James Withers, Aaron Fletcher, John Kines.
(Page 17)

REDMON, JOHN
Inventory. 25 July, 1796.
Aprs: William Barker, Edward Burgess, Mark Shumate.
(Page 23)

Dower of Wilky Duncan, widow of John Duncan, dec'd.
Moses Duncan, administrator of estate. Milly Duncan, heir of John Duncan, dec'd. July 25, 1796.

EMMONS, WILLIAM
5 February, 1795. 25 July, 1796.
All estate to wife during widowhood.
Daughter, Agattha Emmons, to have personal property.
After decease of wife all property to be sold and divided among all the children.
Exrs: son Joseph and William Jones (son-in-law)
Wit: Peter Grant, Thomas Keith, John Wooden. (Page 27)

WINN, MINOR
Inventory. 26 February, 1796.

BILLINGSLEY, CLEMENT
Inventory. 24 October, 1796
Apprs: Mathew Neale, Joseph Smith, L. Mallory. (Page 32)

RAMSDELL, MAJOR THOMAS
Inventory. October, 1796.
Apprs: Samuel Steele, George Rogers, Joseph Hale. (Page 33)

TALBUT, JOHN
12 April, 1796. 24 October, 1796
Wife, Ann, to have slaves during lifetime.
Daughter, Ann, to have slaves.
Son John, to have slaves.
A tract of land in Prince George County, Maryland, to be sold and the money to be divided among wife and 4 children.
Exrs: wife and son Benjamin.
Wit: John Wrenn, Samuel Dennis, Isaac Wrenn. (Page 35)

KERR, JOHN
8 Nov. 1796. 26 Dec. 1796
Daughter, Margaret Bronaugh, 5 pounds curr. and other gifts.
Daughter, Mary Peters, 1 Negro.
Daughter, Betty Kerr, 2 Negroes.
Sons, John Kerr, Jr. and William Kerr, each to have a slave.
Wife, Sarah, to have use of estate during life.
Children: Sarah Crosby Kerr, William Kerr, Dorcas Kerr, Lucy Kerr, Peggy Smith Kerr and Asenth Kerr. (Some of the above mentioned children were by a first wife)
Exrs: wife, John Withers, John James.
Wit: Benjamin Bronaugh, Garrett Freeman, James Fox.
(Page 36)

MOREHEAD, SAMUEL
17 December, 1796
Daughters, Lydia, Mary, Elizabeth and Peggy Morehead, to have slaves.
Slaves to sons, Charles and Samuel Morehead.
Grandson, Baylor Jennings, a slave.
Wife, Wilmarth, all estate during her widowhood.
Exrs: wife, Thomas Helm, Charles Morehead.
Wit: Thomas Humston, John Morehead, Isaac Eustace. (Page 47)

GEORGE, PARNACH
Inventory. 24 February, 1797

FOLEY, JAMES
14 October, 1793. 24 April, 1797
Wife, Elizabeth, all estate during widowhood.
Children by wife Elizabeth - Susannah, Oglovio P., Oglivio Loah, Oglovio Lottice, Molly. Son Enoch.
Other children: John James, Thomas William, Bryant, Sarah Watts, Enoch Foley.
Exrs: wife and son Enoch.
Exrs: Alexander Keith, Hnry Harris, William Keith, Lottice Thornton.
Wit: Obannon Keith, Henry Harris, Lottice Thornton, Catty Keith.
(Page 55)

OBANNON, JOHN
21 Feb. 1797. 24 April, 1797
Wife, Lydia, to have slaves and land during widowhood.
To son, Joseph, 1/3 of all my land in Kentucky.
Daughter, Elizabeth Smith.
To son, James, 300 pounds of curr.
Daughter Jomina Johnston, slave.
Son, Isham, a slave.
To son, Elias, to have 1/3 of land in Kentucky.
To son, William, residue of land in Fauquier County.
To son, John, 1/3 of land in Kentucky.
Exrs: wife, sons Joseph, James and John.
Wit: William Metcalfe, Alexander Keith, Richard Parker. (Page 52)

CLARK, BENJAMIN
27 November, 1794. 26 June, 1797
Wife, Mary, to have estate during life and at her decease to be divided between children. Children: Thomas, Ann Crupper, Elizabeth Clark, Mary Clark. Grandchildren: children of dau. Cloe Crupper.
Wt: Samuel Pearle, Henry Moore, Henry Downs.
Exrs: wife and son Thomas.
(Page 56)

SLOOTS, JOHN
5 Sept. 1796. 26 June, 1797.

(Con. from page 58)
To wife. Tomsen, land and household goods.
Sons, Leonard, James, Clabourn, Lewis, Enoch, to have 1 shilling each.
Sons, Barton and William, to have 1 pence each.
Daughters, Mary Betsy, Charity and Frances, to have 1 shilling each.
Exr: wife.
Wit: A. Davis, De Wood, William Wood. (Page 58)

DUNCAN, LYDIA
2 October, 1795. 24 June, 1797
To sons, Joseph and Housen Duncan, Negroes.
Daughters, Lydia Obannon (hus. John), Jemina Mauzy (hus. John), Hannah Porter (hus. Ebenezer), each to have slaves.
Exrs: sons Joseph and Housen.
Wit: Enoch Withers, Moses Duncan, John Korr. (Page 66)

CAVE, THOMAS
26 July, 1797. 25 Sept. 1797.
Estate to be equally divided among 4 children : Rhody, John, Sarah and Samuel Cave. They are to receive their share at age of 17 years.
Wit: Joseph Dickman, Philip Cooksey. (Page 67)

HARRISON, BENJAMIN
2 January, 1798. 22 Jan. 1798
To daughter, Margaret Short Wagner, 10 pounds curr.
To David Harrison, 10 pounds and my wearing apparel.
Slave Samuel to be emancipated.
All rest of estate to be given grandson, Benjamin Harrison Wagner.
Exrs: Col. Peter Wagner, Benjamin Batts, of Dumfries.
Wit: Philip Spille, James Lloyd, Charles Waller. (Page 90)

LAWSON, JOHN
Probated 22 Jan. 1798
Capt. Hancock Lee has a warrant for 840 acres which I wish to be located for the benefit of my creditors. Edward Digges to inherit land after the decease of my wife. (Not named)
Wit: Willy Roy, Edward Digges, Jr. (Page 92)

PICKETT, WILLIAM
10 January, 1798. 26 February, 1798.
To wife, Martha, bedstead, 1 pair of fire dogs.
Son, William, 1 mare & colt, furniture and household goods.
Son James, 1 feather bed and furniture.
Daughter, Ann Pickett, feather bed & furniture, choice of slaves in lieu of Daniel. Daughter Sukey Brady, 1 horse and property in her possession. Children: John, Sanford, William, James, Patty Fishback, Sukey Brady, Molly Jackson, Sally Motcalfe, Ann Pickett, Subroy Smith.
Exrs: sons James and William.
Wit: William Metcalfe, Joseph Smith. (Page 102)

SMITH, WILLIAM
15 Oct. 1789. 26 Feb. 1796.   Hamilton Parish.
Son William and dau. Mary Soddust (?) to have slaves.
Son Andrew to have slaves and stock.
Exrs: son Andrew and James Withers (cousin)
Wit: Thomas Withers, John Withers, Hannah Smith.

HARRISON
Renunciation. Mary Harrison, wife of Benjamin, will not accept any
provision made for her by her late husband. 30 Jan. 1798.
Wit: Ennis Comb, Thomas Gibson, Joseph George. (Page 109)

MATHEWS, JOHN
Schoolmaster. 24 February, 1798. 28 July, 1798.
To Mary, dau. of Josias Fishback, a tract of land containing 500 acres,
being in the County of Lincoln in State of Kentucky.
To William Blackwell (son of Col. John Blackwell) a horse & bridle.
After payment of funeral expenses money is to be divided between Sarah
Battaile Fitzhugh, Dudley Fitzhugh (children of William Fitzhugh of
Prospect Hill) and Mary Fitzhugh (dau. of George Fitzhugh of Turkey Run).
Exrs: Col. John Blackwell, of Tinpot, William Fitzhugh, of Prospect
Hill and George Fitzhugh of Turkey Run. (Page 128)

JOHNSON, ISAAC
9 June, 1798. 23 July, 1798
Wife, Lydia, to have 2 slaves and lease of land where I now live.
After decease of wife brother Baldwin Johnson shall possess all
estate.
Exrs: John Smith and his son Thomas.
Wit: Isaac Neigh, Ann Neigh, Dosha Crim, William Griffin.

ROUSAN, WILLIAM
19 July, 1792. 25 July, 1798
Wife Priscilla to have land during her life, at her decease to be divided
between 3 children   - Henry, Margaret Combs, Nancy Peters.
Sons, John, William (wife Lydia), Henry (wife Sarah).
Grandson, William Rousan (son of William), a Negro.
Daughter Margaret Comb (wife of Ennis), a Negro.
Dau. Susannah Payne and husband, Benjamin Payne, to have possession
of a Negro. Daughter Nancy and husband, John Peters, to have a Negro
woman. Gr.dau. Betsy Karr, to have slave after decease of wife.
Exrs: wife, son Henry, Ennice Combs. (Page 130)

PICKETT, WILLIAM SANDFORD
Inventory. 28 Jan. 1799
(Page 146)

SINKLAR, WILLIAM
24 Jan. 1798. ----
After decease of wife land is to be sold and divided among the children James, John, Isaac, Archibald, William, Middleton, Horatio, Elisabeth Jones, Nancy and Mary Fogan (hus. Edward).
Exrs: wife (Lydia), sons James and John.
Wit: William Metcalfe, Charles Barnett, George Payne, Joshua Kennard.
(Page 137)

DAVIS, CHARLES
16 May, 1796. 24 Sept. 1798
Wife Lydia to have est. to during life and widowhood.
Daughters, Lucy Wheat and Lydia Davis.
Sons: Griffith, Charles, William, Levi, Richard and John.
Two granddaughters - Elizabeth Davis, Elizabeth Davis, personal property. Exrs: Sons, Griffith, Charles, William.
Wt: James H. Bookman, Gerrard Keating, Jemina Keating. (Page 140)

SANFORD, RICHARD
2 Sept. 1798. 22 Oct. 1798
Wife Betty to have estate during widowhood.
Sons: Robert, John, William, Bennett.
Exrs: wife, Robert Sanford (son), James Hunton, Richard Baker.
Wit: Hannah Hunton, Bernard Duffy, Owen Thomas, Thomas Hunton.
(Page 145)

KEMPER, JOHN
2 Feb. 1796. 25 Feb. 1799
Wife, Ann, to have land where she now lives, during widowhood.
Son, Peter, horse & bridle and land in Culpepper County.
Son, Moses, to have horse. Dau. Susannah Hardistrees, 5 pounds curr.
Son, John, 100 acres of land in Culpepper County.
Sons, Charles, Joseph and Elias, each to have a horse and bridle.
Daughters: Catey, Elizabeth, Susannah, Mary, Anney Kemper.
Son Tilman Kemper. Estate to be divided equally among children.
Exrs: sons, Peter, John, Charles, Joseph.
Wit: Jacob Kemper, Sr., Jacob Kemper, Jr. (Page 153)

THOMAS, WILLIAM
14 Nov. 1798. 22 April, 1799.
All estate to wife, Allenner, except that bequeathed the following children: Daniel, Eramus, John, William (last 2 are the youngest).
Daughters, Rebecca and Precious, to have slaves and furniture.
Exrs: wife, sons Daniel and William.
Wit: Reuben Strother, Richard Turner, James Channel. (Page 176)

MALLORY, CLEMENT F.
Inventory. --1800. (Page 222)

WINKFIELD, HONOR
24 Nov. 1798. 22 April, 1799
To Bon, a Negro slave, belonging to James Gillison, Sr., whom I claim
as my husband, all my estate.
Exrs: John Gillison, Lewis Shumate.
Wit: Elizabeth Shumate, Betty Shumate, Jane Shumate. (Page 177)

BUCHANAN, MICHAEL
15 January, 1799. 24 June, 1799
Brother, John Buchanan and Aquilla Janny, of Berkeley County, are appointed executors, they are to give 1000 acres of land that I purchased in the Northwest Territory of Dr. Solden, to my nieces, Mary and Hannah Buchanan (daus. of bro. Thomas, dec'd), of Pennsylvania.
Aquilla Janny to have 100 acres and $200. for his kindness.
Wit: Hezekiah Glascock, William McEndress (?). (Page 181)

RECTOR, HENRY
8 Jan. 1799. June 1799.
Son, Elijah, to have 35 pounds curr.
Daughter, City, 12 pounds curr; her dau. Polly to have personal property.
Son Spencer and his children- Edward, John, Henry, Mary Ann, Poncey (or Percy). Wit: Joseph Lloyd, Hezekiah Glascock, William Finch. (Page 182)

PORTER, THOMAS
10 May, 1799. 24 June, 1799
Son, Eli, to have 150 acres of land. Daughter, Betty Porter.
Children who are married : Hannah Jackman, Sarah Scott, John Porter, William, Thomas, Charles and Edwin Porter.
Wearing clothes to be divided among my servants, Jack, Will and Sam:
Exrs: sons, William, Thomas. (Page 184)

BROWN, JONATHAN
19 May, 1799. 22 July, 1799.
To wife, Mary Brown, whole of estate for her use and disposal forever.
Wit: Samuel Chilton, William Brown, James Seaton, Betty Konner.
(Page 188)

ROCKHARD, THOMAS
8 August, 1788. July, 1799
"Wife to have estate during widowhood, unless she makes waost with any part of estate then she forfeits the above gift."
Daughter Nancy and her son, Robert Carter Rockhard. Dau. Lydia Aden to have 1 shilling. Grandchildren, Hiram and Elizabeth Rockhard, to have 1/2 of estate. Exrs: wife Sarah and George Calvert.
Wit: James Weeks, George Walker, Richard Cochran. (Page 189)

Sale of Estate of Joseph Barbee. 27 Jan. 1800. (Page 225)

THORNBURY, JOHN
3 November, 1795. 23 September, 1799
Wife, Elizabeth Thornbury.
Sons, Henry, Samuel and Francis, to have plantation where they now live.
Daughters, Peggy Myers and Mary Wigginton.
Children: Henry, Daniel, Samuel, Francis, William, Thomas, Peggy, Mary, Zachariah and Elisabeth.
"Have a patent in 1700 acres of land in Kentucky."
Exs: sons Samuel, Francis and William.
Wit: Henry Dade Hooes, Moses Moss, Thomas Green.
(Page 196)

An Account of estate of James Stewart, dec'd. James Stewart, Jr. Exr.
Apprs: Charles Marshall, Thomas Diggs, Willy Roy, S. Duffy.
(Page 212)

LUCKETT, THOMAS
6 January, 1800. 21 January, 1800
Sons, John, Douglas, Thomas, William, to have 3 pounds and 2 shillings each, that was left them by their aunt Elisabeth.
Son Richard to have 17 pounds curr.
Daughters, Cloe Tongue, Elenor Cox, Nancy and Mary.
Exrs: son Ignatus, James Cox, Joshua Tongue.
Wit: Daniel Orear, John Peters, Samuel Cave.
(Page 219)

GIBSON, JONATHAN
27. January, 1800
(Page 227)

Sale of estate of Thomas Porter.
24 February, 1800. Exrs: William, Thomas and Edwin Porter. (Page 239)

EDMONDS, JOHN, JR.
1 September, 1798. 18 September, 1798. Nuncupative.
(Died Tuesday, 8 August, 1798)
Proved by the oath of William Edmonds.
Land to be equally divided among, William, George, John, Elias and Peggy. Property intended for Nancy, wife of William Blackwell, to be left in trust for her. William Blackwell to have nothing. (Page 244)

BRADFORD, DANIEL
16 January, 1800. 25 April, 1800. Hamilton Parish.
Slaves to sons, John, William and Charles. Sons, Enoch and Fielding, a tract of land in Kentucky, where they now live.
Son, Simon, 250 acres in Fauquier County and tract of land in Kentucky.
Daughters, Mary Allen, Violetta Bradford, Sarah and Katy, land.
Exrs: wife (not named), sons, William and Simon.
Wit: Benjamin Edwards, John Estham (or Eastham). (Page 246)

BRENT, WILLIAM
13 February, 1793. 23 June, 1800
To wife, Hannah Brent, estate for life, 11 slaves and household goods.
After decease of wife the estate to go to sons, Christopher Noale Brent
and George Brent.   Children: Thomas, William, Alexander, Christopher
Noale, George, Ann, Mary Waddy Brent and Elizabeth Mary Brent.
Exrs: wife, Thomas Brent, William Brent, David Blackwell.   (Page 258)

BUSSEY, CORNELIAS
13 February, 1800. 23 September, 1800
To wife, Jane Bussey, all estate during life.
Mentions children but does not name, except daughter, Peggy Bragg (hus.
Dessor Bragg). Wit: William Adams, Walter Adams, Richard Woll. (P. 263)

HACKLEY, LOTT
4 March, 1798. 25 June, 1798.
Wife, Jael(or Joel) to have estate, wife to decide whether slaves are to
be free, if they are kept they are to be divided among brothers and sisters at decease of wife. Mention is made of brother Francis Hackley, sister Lucy Johnson, Mary Underwood, Samuel Reed (bro.-in-law) and Mildred
Stigler (wife of James Stigler). Exrs: wife, James Stigler, Thomas Keith.
Wit: Peter Grant, Thomas Peyton, Daniel Hickson.   (Page 264)

CUNDIFF, ISAAC
4 July, 1796. 22 September, 1800
Wife, Lettes Cundiff, to have estate during her life time;
Children: James, Betty Laws, Sally Feagins, Lucy Roberson, Winny Furr.
Exrs: wife, John Laws (son-in-law)
Wit: Benjamin Carpenter, Margaret Barten, Joseph Jefferson, Jr., John
Feagan, William Furr. (Page 265)

Dr. Charles Chilton Estate. Admrs: Joseph Blackwell, Thomas Chilton,
27 October, 1800. (Page 272)

BOWERS, PETER
15 October, 1800. 22 December, 1800
Son, Michael, to receive 5 pounds curr.
Gr.daughter, Susan Bowers (dau. of Michael), slave.
Son, William, to have land, slave and surveying instruments.
Daughter, Molly, to have 5 pounds curr. and her children to have land
and slave. Granddaughter, Betsy Glendenning.
Daughter, Rachel, to receive 60 pounds curr.
Daughter, Rosannah, to have slaves and land, to have support through
life. Daughter Peggy's children to have 5 pounds curr.
Daughter Betsy to live with daughter Molly.
Exrs: James Wright, Williams Bowers, Peter Connoy.
Wit: Joseph King, Elizabeth King and Henry King.
(Page 277)

GIBSON, ABRAHAM
October 27, 1800. --;----
Wife, Ann Gibson, to have estate during life and widowhood.
Children: Mary Barnes, Nancy Yates, Jane Strother, Elisabeth Davis, Jacob, Frances Yates (formerly Frances Holtzclaw, lately intermarried with Lewis Yates), Sarah Lambert.
Exrs: Ann Gibson, Lewis Yates.
Wit: Hugh Chinn, William Yates, Joseph Cross. (Page 292)

EUSTACE, WILLIAM
7 December, 1800. 23 February, 1801.
Wife Ann to have slaves and estate during life.
Son, Hancock, to have land where I now live, all furniture except what I have given his mother. Son, William, to have 2 slaves.
    John Gibson (or Gilson), grandson.
Daughter Mary and son William.
Wit: Thomas Blackwell, Samuel Blackwell, William Jones.
    (Page 293)

PINKARD, WILLIAM
25 April, 1798. 23 February, 1801
All estate to wife, Mildred, and to be disposed of at her decease among the children as she thinks proper.
Wit: Cornelius Bussey, Richard Woll.
(Page 294)

HANSON, ANN
6 April, 1800. 3 October, 1800
(Ann Hanson was formerly from Charles. County, Maryland)
Son, Sam Claggett, to have land I bought of my son, Gustavus. Brown Hornor, 300 acres, in another tract 114 acres. I give Samuel the above property as an act of justice as he has sustained much loss by my two marriages. Grandson, William Edward Hornor (son of William). Mentions former husband, Robert Hornor. Sons, William and John Hornor. Susanne W. Harris, granddaughter of late husband, Samuel Hanson, is needy, to be given 50 pounds curr, but money not to be under control of her husband. Gold sleeve buttons to Ann Hanson, daughter of Col. Samuel Hanson, of Georgetown. Granddaughters: Frances, Elisabeth and Catherine Hornor. Exrs: Samuel Claggett, Gustavus Brown Hornor, William Hornor.
Wit: Ann Ireland Brown, G.R. Brown, Gustavus Brown, Jr.
(Page 299)

MCNEEL, JOHN
4 June, 1784. 22 June, 1801
Legatees: Sarah Ball (wife of David), 170 acres of land - "she and her ayers."
Wit: Anne Ball, Benjamin Ball, William D. Darnall.
(Page 306)

NICKOLS, THOMAS
27 March, 1801.   27 July, 1801   Of Parish of Leeds.
Wife, Mary to have entire estate.
Son of brother James Nickols, by name of Nathan, to have 1 shilling.
Exrs: wife and Charles Adams.
Wit: Gregory Glasscock, Carly Adams, Nancy Adams.
(Page 317)

CRAIG, JAMES
2 July, 1792.   22 June, 1801
Slaves to be liberated.
Samuel Holiday to have 400 pounds of curr.
Jane Stewart (widow of James) to have 5 pounds in case she survives me,
if she does not the same amount to her daughter, Betty.
Jane Smith, widow of Alexander Smith, 5 pounds currency.
Mrs. Williams, mother-in-law of Cossum Day, to have 5 pounds curr.
Bequest to children of John and Margaret Doby, their son James excepted.
Legatees: Joseph Craig (brother), James Doby and wife, Ann.
Exrs: Gavin Lawson (of Stafford County) and William Allanson (of Fauquier
County), each to receive 50 pounds curr.
Wit: Edward Pendleton, Daniel Morgan, William Lawson, Daniel Wheatley.
(Page 303)

DULIN, WILLIAM
18 June, 1801.   27 July, 1801
To son, William Dulin, 5 pounds currency.
Daughter, Elizabeth Welch, 40 pounds currency.
Son, John, to have 25 pounds curr.
Son, Edward, to have 50 pounds curr.
Son, Philip, to have 50 pounds curr.
Son, Charles, to have 3 pounds of curr.
Son, George, to have 7 slaves.
Daughter, -- Glascock Clemence.
Grandson, George Dulin (son of William)
Grandson, William Elsey Dulin.
Elizabeth Haddox Dulin, feather bed.
Exrs: wife (Clemence) and son George.
Wit: James W. Fishback, Gregory Glascock, David W. Morris.
(Page 319)

JONES, WILLIAM
25 July, 1793.   22 December, 1800
Wife, Mary, to have estate during widowhood.
Daughters, Sarah and Hannah.
Daghters, Cary and Lucretia, to receive as much as first children when
they married.   Exrs: sons James and William.
Wit: Septimus Norris, John Norris.   (Page 320)

HANSBOROUGH, GABRIEL
8 December, 1799.   28 July, 1800.   (Con. on page 67)

Wife, Molly Hansborough.
Mentions two sons, James and Peter.
Exrs: Peter Conway, Nathaniel Graves, John Peters.

MASSIE, THOMAS
20 October, 1801. 28 December, 1801.
Wfe, Dolly Massie.
Daughter, Mary Triplett.
Children: Asa, Thomas, Samuel, Josias, Benjamin Morehead, John.
Son Robert Massie, Dollie and Nimrod Massie, to have slaves made over to them by John Morehead.
Son, Asa, to have 100 acres of land in Kentucky.
Exrs: wife, son Asa, Joseph Chilton.
Wit: Joseph Chilton, Edward Shacklett, John Cooke, Joseph Smith.
(Page 339)

LEWIS, JAMES
21 January, 1802. 26 January, 1802.
Estate lately received from James Lewis (uncle) of Spottsylvania County, to go to wife, Jane. All estate that comes from father to go to brother, William Lewis. Exr: brother William Lewis.
Wit: George Pickett, Charles Marshall, James Walker.
(Page 347)

SKINKER, THOMAS
1 March, 1801. 26 April, 1802.
Legatees: Ephiram Abell, John Hickerson, Samuel Skinker (son of bro. William) to have land in Stafford County, William Skinker (son of bro. Samuel). William Skinker (nephew).
(Page 354)

HINSON, ROBERT
29 March, 1802. 26 April, 1802.
Elisabeth Whitton to receive $20. per month.
Daughter, Ann Dialls (or Dealls), all children not named.
Exrs: James Hinson, Tapley Hinson (sons)
Wit: John Blackwell, John Bronaugh, Thomas Blackwell.
(Page 355)

BROOKS, HUMPHREYS
7 April, 1802; 24 May, 1802
Wife, Milly, to have use of plantation during widowhood, slaves and silver.
Sons, Francis and Mathew Whiting Brooks.
Daughters: Ann Brooks, Catherine Powell, Lucy Igram, Elisabeth Diggas.
Exrs: Mathew Whiting Brooks (son) and Burr Powell (son-in-law).

NORRIS, WILLIAM
15 December, 1801. 26 April, 1802. (Cont on page 68)

Estate to be divided into twelve equal parts.
Sons: John, Joseph, Samuel and William.
Daus: Elizabeth, Hannah, Ellin, Sarah, Mary, Catherine, Nancy Bailey.
Grandchildren: children of daughter, Susannah Robinson.
Exrs: sons, John and Joseph Norris.
Wit: William Barker, Charles Barker, Presley Hampleton.
(Page 357)

JAMES, JOHN
8 September, 1801. 25 April, 1802.
Wife, Elizabeth James.
Children: Mary, Margaret, Aldridge and David.
Exrs: sons Aldridge and David, James Wright.
Wit: Peter Conway, Britain Lewis, John Shumate, Sr.
(Page 387)

HUME, ANDREW
20 March, 1802. 24 May, 1802.
Children: Robert, Andrew, John, George and Hannah Hume.
Exrs: sons Andrew and George.
Wit: James Wood, Zaachous Quisenberry, Henry Wardon.
(Page 382)

SPENNY, WILLIAM
11 May, 1802. 24 May, 1802.
Estate to brother, Benjamin Spenny.
Exr: brother Benjamin Spenny (or Sperry)
Wit: Nathaniel Rector, Charles Pickett, Eppa Timberlake.
(Page 382)

MCFARLAND, JOHN
Legatees: John McFarland (nephew) and children of Robert McFarland (brother). Extrx: wife Jane McFarland.
Wit: James Batson, Jesse McVeigh, M. Lacy.
(Page 346)

KERNES, WILLIAM
18 December, 1799. 27 September, 1802.
Daughters, Elizabeth Stadler and Ann Kernes.
Sons: John, Daniel, William, John M. and Benjamin Horton Kernes.
Exr: son John Kernes.
Wit: James Wright, Benjamin Horton, Augustine Horton, Samuel Elliott.
(Page 397)

TOMPKINS, JOHN
25 June, 1802. 22 November, 1802.
At present at the home of Mr. Samuel Stooles, in Fauquier County.
Wife to receive $2,000. (Not named)
Mention is made of brother, Fontanatus Tompkin and other brothers and sisters. Exrs: Christopher Tompkins and Henry Tompkins (bros.)
Wit: George Rogers and Ann Garner. (Page 403)

WINN, JOHN
18 August, 1801. 24 January, 1803.
Wife, Mary Winn.
Children: Mary, John Smallwood, Thomas Roley, Zachary Cox, John Noble, Elisabeth Lombard, Sarah Ann, Hester V. Grandson, Daniel Gellerson.
Exrs: wife and son Thomas.
Wit: Walter Oliver, Enoch Jameson, James Cox.
(Page 419)

HAMPTON, JOSEPH
15 October, 1802. 28 February, 1803.
Wife, Molly Hampton.
Children: John, Lawson, Jeremiah, Susannah, Joseph, Francis and Alfred.
Exrs: wife, Richard Nutt, Thomas Weeks.
Wit: Burr Powell, Elisabeth Batson, Winny Nutt, Minny Hampton. (Page 423)

PEYTON, YELVERTON
Probated 28 February, 1803.
Son, Yelverton Peyton.
Wife, Margaret C. Peyton (formerly Scott).
Mentions brother, Richard Henry Peyton.
The will was proven by the oaths of Chandler Peyton, John Scott, Charles Marshall. (Page 424)

CHADWELL, JOHN
27 November, 1799. 23 ----, 1803.
Wife, Elizabeth Chadwell.
Estate to be divided among my first children.
Exrs: wife, William Guttridge.
Wit: Alexander Monroe, Thomas White, Elijah Gutridge.
(Page 431)

COX, ABRAHAM
1 February, 1803. 25 July, 1803.
Wife, Elizabeth Cox.
Daughters: Mary Winn, Ann, Elizabeth Cox (dau.-in-law)
Sons: Thomas, William, Zachariah Cox.
Exrs: wife, Zachariah Cox (son), James Cox (gr.son). (Page 436)

SMITH, ENOCH
6 October, 1803. 25 July, 1803
Wife, Elizabeth Smith
Sons: John (eldest), Elijah, Hedgman, Isham, Elias.
Daughter, Lucinda. Unborn child.
Exrs: wife, John Smith (son), John Obannon, William Obannon.
Wit: James Elias and William Obannon. (Page 437)

HEFLIN, WILLIAM
21 April, 1803. 25 July, 1803.
Wife mentioned, but not named.
Son: William Heflin.
Daughters: Larkey, Polly and Anna.
Exrs: Elijah Arnold, William Heflin, Jr.
Wit: Chapman Grant, Mitchell Bird.
(Page 439)

JOHNSTON, MOSES, SR.
16 June, 1803. 25 July, 1803. Of Parish of Leeds.
Wife: Duanna Johnston.
Sons: Moses, Daniel, David, Nimrod, John.
Daughters: Molly, Susannah Waddle, Margaret McMecklin, Charlotte Johnston. Exrs: Am-----Bailey, Simon Cornwell.
Wit: James Ellis, Joseph Ellis, Isham Obannon.
(Page 440)

HITT, PETER
17 August, 1802. 25 October, 1802.
Wife, Hannah Hitt.
Children: Presley, Harrison, Alexander, Mary, Susannah, Thaddeus, Nancy, Fanny, Elizabeth and unborn child.
Unless wife remarries estate not to be divided until her decease.
Exrs: son Pressley and Gabriel Green (of Culpepper County).
(Page 440)

WOOD, DICKERSON
23 January, 1803. 25 July, 1803.
Wife, Mary Wood.
Sons: Dickerson, William, Elijah, James.
Mentions a daughter, but does not name.
Wit: Lewis Jones, Enoch Smoot. (page 441)

SEATON, JOHN
Probated 24 October, 1803.
Wife, Alice Seaton.
Mention is made of estate left by father, James Seaton.
Children: James, Francis, Lydia, George, John and William.
Exr: Rouben Murray.

ASH, FRANCIS
17 February, 1800. 24 October, 1803.
Wife, Nancy Ash.
Children: Sarah, Elisabeth, Thornton, Susannah, Maria, Lucy, Kitty, Harriott, John Richard and Juliet.
Exrs: Thomas Adams, William Ash (brother).
Wit: Cornelius King, Orphy King, John A. Bolling.   (Page 466)

KEARTON, ANTHONY
18 May, 1803.   24 October, 1803.
Wife, Fanny Kearton.
Legatees: brothers, John and Thomas Kearton and sister Elizabeth.
Exrs: Richard Baker, Thaddeus Norris, Charles Marshall.
(Executors refuse to act.)   (Page 467)

WAKE, ROBERT
6 July, 1803. September, 1803.
Legatees: brother, William and mother.
Extrx: Mary Wake (mother).
(Page 468)

BURKE, WILLIAM
17 May, 1803. 26 December, 1803
Wife, Susannah, to have lease of land in Fairfax County.
Children: Jane, Sarah, John, George, Elizabeth, Polly, William, Susan and Ann Burke.
Wit: Jesse Tharp, Henry Benard.   (Page 481)

WITHERS, WILLIAM
21 November, 1803. 23 January, 1804.
To son, James Withers, a tract of land in Culpepper County.
Son, Spencer Withers.
Daughters, Susan, Elizabeth Withers (wife of John Withers).
Daughter, Molly Withers (wife of William Withers).
Daughter, Alese Withers (wife of John Ball.)
Daughter, Agatha, wife of Martin Porter.
Son, Jesse Withers, to have land willed to testator by his father.
Sons, Lewis and Elijah Withers. Granddaughter, Betty Withers (dau. of William).   Exrs: sons, James, Jesse and Lewis Withers.
Wit: Enoch Withers, Mathew Withers, Jonnotto Withers.
(Page 492)

JAMES, BENJAMIN
27 September, 1803. 23 January, 1804.
Wife, Elizabeth James.
Sons, Benjamin, Thomas and John.
Exrs: wife, son Benjamin and cousin Joseph James.

CURTICE, JOHN
8 February, 1802. 24 January, 1804.
Legatees: Susannah Stigler (or Steggers), "my companion", to have all of estate, after her decease it is to be equally divided between the following: John Stigler, alias Curtice ; Lewis Stigler alias Curtice; Elijah Steigler alias Curtice. "Only sons Susannah Stigler has had by me." Daughters: Elizabeth and Lucy Stiglers.
Exrs: William Hampton, William Hunton.
(Page 495)

MAUZY, HENRY
31 December, 1799. 27 February, 1804.
Wife, Elizabeth Mauzy.
Children: John, Nancy Bayse, Henry, Peter, William, Priscilla Roper, George, Ethel Newman, Susannah Komper, Thomas, Richard, Michael and Joseph. Exrs: wife, Thomas, Richard and Michael and Joseph.
James Peters (son-in-law) and his ten children that he had by daughter Betty Mauzy.

PICKETT, MARTIN
4 May, 1803. 25 April, 1804.
Daughters, Lucy Marshall (hus. Charles), Letty Johnson, Milly Clarkson. Judah Slaughter (hus. Stanton), Betsy, Nancy Brooke (hus. Francis)
Sons: George Blackwell Pickett and Steptoe Pickett.
Brothers: John and William Pickett.
All land in Kentucky bequeathed to five daughters.
Exrs: son George Pickett, Gen. John Blackwell, Stanton Slaughter.
(A long will)   (Page 519)

CHUNN, JOHN THOMAS
31 January 1804. 28 May, 1804.
Wife, but not named.
Legatees: children of sister Henrietta Turner; children of sister, Charity Edwards; Zach Vowells; children of dec'd. nephew, Henry Vowels; children of sister, Elizabeth Dyson; children of dec'd. sister, Winnifred Dyson; nephew, John Thomas Chunn; children of dec'd. brother, Zach Chunn; nephew Charles Chunn; friend, Charles Marshall.
Exrs: wife, Zach Vowel (nephew), Andrew Chunn, Zephanic Turner.
Wit: Charles Marshall, Nimrod Ashby.
(Page 527)

MALLORY, CLEMENT
Inventory.   1800   (Page 222)

BARBEE, JONATHAN
27 January, 1800.   Sale of estate.   (Page 225)

ALLISON, WILLIAM
24 May, 1793. 28 April, 1800
To daughter, Mary Semour Hall Allison, at present wife of Robert Rose, to have a tract of land equal to 500 acres that came to me by her worthy mother, now deceased, and another large tract of land of about 1000 acres. Daughter's present husband, Robert Rose, is not entitled to any of legacy.
Exr: David Allison (brother)
(Page 249)

YOUNG, JAMES
4 June, 1796. 25 February, 1799
To grandson, James Neale, to have 6 Negroes during life and at his decease they are to be divided between his sons, Richard and William.
To daughter, ----Jones, 5 shilling.
Philip Fishback, to have 32 pounds curr.
To grandson, James Dale, to have wearing apparel.
Mentions 2 daughters, --- Neale and -- Dale and their children.
Exrs: Francis Whiting, James Neale, W. Fitzhugh, W. Fitzhugh.
(Page 255)

MOXLEY, JEREMIAH
Wife, Hannah Moxley.
Daughter, Sebella Moxley, dau. Hannah Moxley (mentions her grandfather, Morris). Sons: James and Solomon.
Exr: Sanders Morris.
9 October, 1803. 27 February, 1804.

END OF BOOK "S".

WILLS FROM MISCELLANEOUS COURT ORDERS -- FAUQUIER COUNTY, VIRGINIA.

WAUGH, MARY
27 March, 1749. 14 December, 1756. Stafford County.
To son, William Mountjoy, large Bible, table, 40 acres of land.
To son, Peter, 300 acres of land in Prince William County, where Francis Watts now lives.
To daughter, Elisabeth Conway, 150 acres of land, after her decease to her son, John Markham, should he die without heirs, then to grandson, Peter Conway. Mentions grandson, Thomas Conway.
To daughter, Mary Donphan, personal estate.
Wit: Michael Bryan, Winifred Ryan, Raleigh Traverse, John Mauzy, Jr.

MAUZY PETER
12 February, 1750. 11 June, 1751
To son Michael, to have part of land where I now live, after decease of loving wife, Elizabeth Mauzy.
Son, Peter Mauzy. Son, John, to have land in Prince William County.
Daughters, Mary Mauzy and Elisabeth Mauzy.
Appoints the following friends to bind out sons until they are 21 years of age: William Mountjoy, Alexander Donphan, John Mauzy, Jr.
Extrx: wife.
Wit: Adam Stephen, John Mauzy, John Petcher (?). Stafford County.

ALLEN, WILLIAM
16 August, 1739; 12 May, 1741.
Of Stafford County, Overwharton Parish.
Mentions land left by Margaret Janaway, dec'd., unto her grandchildren, William and Margaret Lunsford (brother and sister).
Wife, Margaret Allen.
Legatees: John Crump; Sarah Walton (dau.) to have slaves ; gr.son, William Walton (son of William); gr.dau. Ann Walton (father, William Walton).
Daughter, Elizabeth Walter (hus. George) and son, William Walter.
Daughter, Margaret, to have land in Prince William County.
Daughter, Dinah James (hus. John) to have slaves and land in Prince William County, on Elk Run.
Daughter, Hannah Withers, and son, James Withers, to have slaves.
Wife and son William to have plantation where I now live.
Grandson, John Allen.
Exrs: wife and son William.
Wit: Richard Young, John Tibbs, Darly Murphy.

CRUMP, JOHN
27 October, 1744.   23 June, 1746.
Of Hamilton Parish, Prince William County, Virginia.
Daughters: Elisabeth Blackwell, Susannah Hewlett, Hannah Crump.
Sons, George and John, to each have 10 shillings.
Son, Joseph, to have a tract of land in Northumberland County and
8 Negroes.   Estate to be divided when Benjamin arrives at the age of
21 years.
Wit: Lazarus Taylor and William Coale.

SINKLERS, SAMUEL
24 January, 1752.   6 February, 1752
Of Hanover County, Virginia.
Sons, Samuel, John, Thomas, William and George,   ---- land and
slaves.   Mention is made of a tract of land where Daniel Taylor now
lives as one of the tenants.
Money for the education of grandson, John Simpson.
Daughter, Sarah Sinkler, to have 100 pounds of curr. on day of marriage.
Exrs: wife Dinah, sons Samuel and Thomas Sinkler.
Wit: T. Turner, William Cope and Mary Simpson.

MARRIAGE BONDS

Abell, Ephiram	Stringfellow, Betsy	Jan. 14, 1784
Adams, Charles	Furr, Nancy	Jan. 8, 1786
Adams, Gavin	Miller, Susannah	March 4, 1790
Adams, George	Turner, Anna	June 8, 1769
Adams, John	McCormack, Betsy	July 25, 1785
Alexander, Ellis	Phillips, Drusilla	October 21, 1791
Aford, William	Suttle, Fanny	Jan. 14, 1786
Allen, Henry	Nelson, Betty	June 27, 1772
Allen, Henry	McKonkey, Catherine	December 14, 1781
Allen, Azariah	Leach, Sarah	December 24, 1794
Allen, William	Bradford, Mary	December 8, 1764
Allen, William	Pepper, Hannah	August 4, 1781
Allen, John	Snelling, Hannah	July 13, 1786
Allen, ----	Heflin, Sally	March 22, 1787
Ambler, David	Monroe, Molly	July 24, 1793
Ambler, William	Colvin, Sarah	October 30, 1790
Anderson, Cornelius	Riddle, Kitty	Sept. 6, 1790
Anderson, Joseph	Freeman, Charlotte	Dec. 11, 1790
Anderson, Theophiles	Lear (Sear), Molly	Oct. 27, 1788
Anderson, Thomas	Anderson, Sally	Dec. 22, 1799
Arnold, Samuel	Wright, Elizabeth	Sept. 5, 1771
Arnold, Isaac	Porter, Mary	Oct. 23, 1771
Arnold, Samuel	Hitch, Rebecca	Sept. 21, 1798
Ardeb, Aaron	Mahoney, Eliza	Oct. 4, 1796
Ash, Uriel	Churchill, Milly	March 4, 1783

Armsmith, William	McBee, Susan	Sept. 14, 1789
Asbury, George	Taylor, Mary	March 14, 1780
Ash, Francis	Adams, Ann	Dec. 20, 1774
Ashby, Benjamin	Ash, Jane	August 2, 1781
Ashby, Nathaniel	Mauzy, Peggy	Dec. 3, 1777
Ashly, Nimrod	Wright, Frances	Nov. 30, 1759
Ashby, John	Huffman, Catherine	Oct. 27, 1783
Ashby, John	Smith, Sarah	August 5, 1799
Ashby, Robert	Walters, Ann	February 26, 1793
Ashby, Robert	Combs, Catherine	April 28, 1783
Ashby, William	Tibbs, Mary	April 24, 1767
Ashton, Lawerence	McBee, Susan	Sept. 14, 1789
Atwell, Francis	McDonald, Mary	Oct. 25, 1768
Athey, Joshua	Hitch, Elizabeth	April 17, 1780
Atwood, John	Robinson, Lucy	June 1, 1790 (or 1794)
Austin, John	Browning, Elizabeth	Oct. 23, 1788
Austin, John	Burgess, Elizabeth	Jan. 20, 1783
Auberry, Thomas	Fletcher, Ann	Dec. 13, 1764
Bailey, Samuel	Anderson(?) HUDSON, Agga	August 8, 1795
Bailey, William	Mays, Nancy	Dec. 22, 1796
Bailey, John	Barnes, Betsy	Jan. 2, 1793
Bailey, Joseph	Newby, Hannah	August 9, 1777
Bailey, William	Eaton, Abigail	April 21, 1798
Bailey, George	Bragg, Phoebe	April 13, 1781
Bailey, Simon	Lunce, Hester	Dec. 4, 1781
Bailey, Thomas	White, Elizabeth	Feb. 28, 1786
Bailey, James	Ball, Sarah	March 6, 1786

Bailey, Thomas	Campbell, Sarah	Jan. 8, 1787
Bailey, Green	Bragg, Mary	Oct. 13, 1788
Bailey, William	Minter, Betty	March 20, 1789
Bailey, Stephen	Lunceford, ----	April 19, 1781
Bale, James	Claypool, Anne	Jan. 20, 1799
Bales, John	Redd, Barbary	April 8, 1788
Balis, Henry	Edmonds, Sophia	Feb. 25, 1787
Balis (Baylis), William	Turner, Elizabeth	May 22, 1780
Ball, Benjamin	Cook, Nancy	Oct. 28, 1794
Ball, William	Creek, Peggy	Dec. 12, 1794
Ball, William	Keas (Keys), Ann	Feb. 9, 1788
Ballenger, Edward	Routt, Hannah	Nov. 29, 1799
Ballard, John	Brown, Mary	Oct. 20, 1785
Barbee, Edward	Woodward, Caty	Dec. 20, 1797
Barbee, Joseph	Withers, Ann	Feb. 2, 1768
Barbee, Joseph	Laurance, Elizabeth	April 28, 1783
Barbee, John	Dyson, Mary	June 24, 1782
Barbee, William	Hickerson, Ann	Jan. 23, 1785
Barker, Charles	Drake, Jean	May 14, 1789
Barker, John	Glascock, Sarah	Dec. 22, 1789
Barnes, John	Shumate, Judith	Oct. 2, 1796
Barnett, Achilles	James, Ann.	Oct. 11, 1788
Barnett, Joseph	Hitt, Mary	Jan. 2, 1789
Barnett, James	Spinney, Mary	Nov. 28, 1796
Barnett, William	Smith, Catherine	Nov. 22, 1790
Barnett, Ambrose	Neavill, Judith	July 18, 1766
Barnough, John	Curtis, Elisabeth	August 1, 1792
Barry, Greenberry	Davis, Frances L.	August 7, 1787

Barry, Willis	Oldacres, Hannah	Feb. 26, 1793
Bartlett, Thomas	Carroll, Sarah	Jan. 2, 1777
Bartlett, John	Bartlett, Ann	April (?) 20, 1780
Bartlett, James	Phillips, Sarah	August 12, 1790
Barton, William	Heflin, Peggy	June 8, 1799
Bates, Robert	Johnson, Betsy	June 20, 1785
Batterson, Robert	Walker, Ann	Nov. 3, 1796
Bayley, William	Newby, Nancy	Feb. 11, 1782
Bayse, Josiah	Sinclair, Sarah	May 22, 1775
Bayse, Isaac	Bashaw, Frances	Jan. 7, 1786
Bayse, Richard	Taylor, Nancy	Dec. 14, 1781
Baxter, John	Briant, Amelia	Nov. 26, 1772
Beatty, John	Shipp, Nancy	March 23, 1785
Beadle (Bedle), John	Ewan, Margaret	March 3, 1795
Benson, Robert	Stringfellow, Ann	Oct. 14, 1788
Benson, Charles	Benson, Franky	May 15, 1781
Benson, Zachariah	Parklow, Sarah	May 11, 1785
Bennett, Sanford	Cremon, Anne	Jan. 14, 1787
Berry, Elijah	Fegan, Susannah	May 9, 1777
Berry, William	Fegan, Clara	May 7, 1777
Berry, George	Conway, Sarah	May 17, 1777
Berry, Thomas	Hampton, Ann	Feb. 15, 1798
Berryman, Benjamin	Bryant, Anna	April 1, 1775
Berryman, Francis	Barr, Elizabeth	March 8, 1788
Billingsley, James	Moreland, Nancy	Nov. 16, 1791
Bishop, Daniel	Leake, Ann	June 25, 1787
Bishop, James	Lake, Cloe	Dec. 13, 1799

Bland, James	Randall, Hannah	Dec. 1, 1788
Blackman, William	Bashaw, Betsy	Sept. 11, 1785
Blackwell, Samuel	Bragg, Mary	Dec. 27, 1788
Blackwell, James	Blackwell, Ann	March 3, 1766
Blackwell, Joseph	Gibson, Ann Grayson	Aug. 14, 1787
Blackwell, Samuel	Gillison, Peggy	Dec. 1, 1780
Blackwell, Thomas	Grant, Judith	Sept. 26, 1781
Blackaby, George	Palmer, Elizabeth	Jan. 22, 1800
Blackerby, Jeduthan	Chamberlayne, Mary	May 13, 1780
Bogers (or Rogers), Rodham	Runnells, Ann	Feb. 1, 1798
Boley, Elijah	Barracks, Asey	August --, 1792
Borain (Borein), Peter	Edmonds, Elizabeth	Jan. 27, 1781
Bowling, Thomas	Brown, Peggy	June 20, 1797
Bowman, George	Duncan, Priscilla	Nov. 19, 1789
Boyd, John	Wright, Milly	Nov. 20, 1785
Boyce, Richard	Helm, Sarah	June 19, 1765
Boyd, Samuel	Brooke, Molly	August 13, 1777
Bragg, Dosier	Bussey, Peggy	Dec. 10, 1790
Bradley, Hugh	Bashaw, Celia	August 4, 1781
Bray, John	McKinsey, Elizabeth	August 6, 1795
Bramlett, William	Laurance, Ann	Dec. 26, 1795
Branthan, Richard	Crump, Frances	Jan. 26, 1781
Bredwell, Teba	Matthew, Polly	-- 30, 1797
Brian, James	Linn, Mary	May 23, 1780
Broadbent, James	Bailey, Sarah	Feb. 26, 1789
Bronaugh, William	Hall (or Hale), Jane	Dec. 26, 1789
Bronaugh, Thomas	Kendall, Lucretia	Feb. 23, 1790

Bowen, James	Bower (?), Rachel	Dec. 17, 1781
Brooke, William	Anner, Eleanor	Nov. 23, 1793
Brooke, George	Marshall, Judy	April 20, 1785
Brown, Thomas	Sanders, Molly	Dec. 29, 1788
Brown, Thomas	Simmons, Katy	March 9, 1793
Brown, John	Hunton, Polly	March 17, 1796
Brown, John	Stringfellow, Dolly	Dec. 3, 1781
Brown, Thomas	Winterton, Sally	Dec. 11, 1781
Brown, Francis	Smith, Elizabeth	Sept. 23, 1783
Brown, William	Parker, Mary	March 19, 1785
Brown, Thomas	Ash, Ann	October 20, 1785
Brown, Robert	Boyd, Molly	May 29, 1786
Bradford, William	Steele, Molly	Dec. 20, 1786
Bradford, Austin	Hard, Elizabeth	Sept. 14, 1787
Bradford, Benjamin	Allen, Ann	Dec. 30, 1784
Brugham, Thomas	Wilson, Elizabeth	March 10, 1787
Bragg, David	Crawley, Margaret	November 17, 1786
Broadhurst, William	Howell (?), Franky	Dec. 31, 1787
Broadhurst, Joseph	Fanbin, Sally	Oct. 1, 1788
Brink, Alexnnder	Sullivan, Elizabeth	Feby. 4, 1788
Bramlett, Henry	Gough, Gladah	Dec. 30, 1785
Bryan, Battaley	Berryman, Elizabeth	May 20, 1777
Burton, James	Singer, Nancy	April 1, 1789
Button (or Bulton), Jacob	Kamper, Sarah	August 5, 1782
Buckley, William Lawerence	Shipps, Mary	Feb. 14, 1785
Butler, William	Shadwell, Eliza	Sept. 15, 1793
Butler, William	James, Margaret	Dec. 17, 1770

Burgess, Edward	Porter, Frances	Nov. 29, 1787
Burdette, William	Chirley, Mary	Dec. 17, 1788
Burdette, Joseph	Smith, Milly	Oct. 23, 1794
Burras, William	Dews (or Deros), Eliz.	Oct. 26, 1797
Byrn, Thomas	Leach, Elizabeth,	Dec. 29, 1785
Callahan, James	Phillips, Elizabeth	Sept. 24, 1787
Calvin, Henry	Williams, Catherine	Dec. 21, 1787
Colvin, William	George, Ann	Dec. 26, 1788
Calmes, Marquis, Jr.	Heale, Priscilla	Feb. 18, 1782
Camack, Henry	Ellis, Molly	May 25, 1790
Camragg, David	Wood, Mary	Dec. 29, 1795
Cameron, Angus	Haley, Ann	Oct. 30, 1794
Campbell, Owen	Settle, Betty	June 15, 1772
Cannon, John	Brazier, Sarah Harrison	Sept. 30, 1782
Canor (?), Mathew	Hinson, Ann	May 25, 1781
Carpenter, Benjamin	McFarlin, Elizabeth	July 20 1788
Carsell, Sanford.	Bartlett, Betty	Feb. 13, 1771
Carter, Isaac	Newstead, Lydia	August 1, 1793
Carter, John	Wood, Mary	Dec. 4, 1780
Carter, Dale	Robinson, Molly	Nov. 23. 1785
Carter, James	Dermont, Sarah	Jan. 3, 1787
Carter, James	Scoggins, Elizabeth	August 30, 1799
Carter, William	Chester, (?), Mary	March 5, 1789
Carthron, John	Boswell, Molly	Feb. 12, 1776
Catlett, John	Routt, Rachel	Jan. 22, 1777
Carvell, James	Jeffries, Lettice	March 24, 1788
Chaddick, Charles	Hainey, Winnifred	Jan. 2, 1774

Chadwell, John	Gutridge, Elizabeth	July 6, 1795
Chewnor, John	Hawkins, Sally	Jan. 28, 1795
Chrisman, George	Ractor, Sally	Feb. 25, 1796
Christian, Martin	Hayes, Betsy	March 23, 1797
Christy, Charles	Smith, Nancy	Dec. 23, 1786
Childs, James	McKonkey, Milly	May 16, 1781
Chilton, Charles	Blackwell. Bettie	Dec. 18, 1760
Chilton, Joseph	Smith, Ann	April 2, 1795
Chinn, Chichester	Withers, Susannah	Jan. 9, 1789
Chinn, Hugh	Ash, Peggy	Dec. 15, 1789
Chinn, Thomas	Moore, Ann H.	Dec. 25, 1789
Chandler, William	Martin, Caty	April 13, 1799
Clarke, John	Ransdell, Mary	Jan. 5, 1789
Clarke, George	Hudnall, Alice	June 29, 1772
Clayton, John	Hurill (?), Elizabeth	June 7, 1764
Clayton, William	Chinn, Elizabeth	Feb. 29, 1788
Clayton, Philip	Churchill, Ann	May 6, 1799
Cockran, Nathan	Keys, Margaret	Dec. 2, 1789
Compton, Richard	Barbee, Anna	March 4, 1799
Conner, William	Greening, Franky	August 9, 1788
Conner, James	Parson, Matilda	Oct. 24, 1796
Coppedge, William	Triplett, Mary	July, 1795
Coppage, John	Raley, Peggy	Oct. 25, 1786
Coppage, William	Really, Sarah	Sept. 17, 1783
Conway, Joseph	Turner, Sarah	July 7, 1788
Collins, Joseph	McClanahan, Jane	Jan. 15, 1796
Corbin, John	Tapps, Molly	Jan. 16, 1799

Cooke, John	Fielding, Nancy	Jan. 31, 1783
Corder, Bulis	Stone, Parsiall	Feb. 18, 1788
Corder, John	Utterback, Caty	Oct. 18, 1800
Courtney, William	Smith, Anna	Jan. 10, 1786
Courtney, James	Embrey, Sarah	Dec. 25, 1794
Cooper, Vincent	Cooper, Mary	Jan. 26, 1785
Cornet, Richard	Bowmer, Polly	Sept. 24, 1793
Cornwell, Jacob	Hayes, Molly	Sept. 7, 1790
Cornwell, Peyton	Elliott, Molly	Jan. 14, 1799
Covert, Martin	Obannon, Susannah	Oct. 22, 1790
Covert, Asa	Hudson, Sarah	Dec. 19, 1799
Cranch, John	Groves, Mary	Feb. 26, 1795
Crafford, George	Humes, Mary	April 12, 1797
Crawford, William	Holder, Susannah	Oct. 7, 1789
Crosby, George	Glasscock, Sally	Sept. 7, 1797
Crosby, George	Peters, Elizabeth	Feb. 8, 1799
Crisman, George	Rector, Sally	Feb. 25, 1796
Crosson, John	Lewis, Acken	July 2, 1788
Crupper, John	Thomas, Ann	Dec. 20, 1788
Cunningham, Timothy	Fishback, Sarah	August 25, 1789
Cummings, Levi	Keys, Naomi	Jan. 18, 1797
Cummins, George	Fullers, Sally	Sept. 11, 1799
Cummins, William	Cornelias, Peggy	June 16, 1793
Curtis, Chester	Giles, Pensela	Sept. 5, 1793
Cummings, Daniel	Sullivan, Sarah	Sept. 28, 1785
Daniel, John	Hardin, Nancy	Jan. 8, 1795
Darnall, Joseph	Ball, Sarah	March 22, 1790

Darnall, William	Monroe, Elizabeth	Dec. 18, 1787
Darnall, Raleigh	Brown, Winnifred	May 5, 1788
Darnall, Joshua	Mauzy, Jemina	Dec. 21, 1798
Darnall, David	Carlin, Milly (or Molly)	Dec. 24, 1799
Davis, James	Monday, Millah	May 30, 1793
Davis, George	Grinnan, Elizabeth	Dec. 17, 1770
Davis, Eli	Bannister, Frances	Feb. 13, 1782
Davis, Levi	Kearns, Lydia	March 14, 1786
Davis, Thomas	Withers, Lucinda	Sept. 23, 1795
Dawson, William	Jenkins, Susannah	August 26, 1799
Day, George	Dennis, Susannah	Sept. 24, 1790
Day, John	Hudnall, Nancy	August 23, 1790
Day, William	Corder, Nelly	Sept. 26, 1785
Dean, John	Pragh, Elizabeth	May 6, 1780
Dearing, Conrad	Black, Nancy	August 31, 1791
De Bell, Lewis	Priest, Elizabeth	Oct. 3, 1799
De Bell, William	Talbert, Ann	March 26, 1799
Dells, John	Maddux, Mary	April 14, 1782
Dennis, Isaac	Walker, Sally	May 24, 1793
Dennison, Henry	Dixon, Jenny	March 21, 1787
Dennally (or Donnelly), Thomas	Carter, Ann	May 17, 1790
Dennison, John	Norman, Sally	March 5, 1795
Devers, William	Johnson, Elizabeth	Dec. 22, 1789
Dermont, William	Williams, Mary	Feb. 21, 1787
Dobin, James	Whitley, Ann	Nov. 26, 1781
Dodd, Daniel	Settle, Hannah	Sept. 13, 1800
Donaldson, Stephens	Boswell, Susannah	June 17, 1782

Donaldson, Daniel	Morehead, Cary	Oct. 30, 1786
Dowdall, Thomas	Wickliffe, Bettie	Feb. 13, 1781
Dowell, Nehemiah	Dearen, Bettie	March 28, 1793
Dowdall, Browner	Humes, Alecy	Jan. 21, 1788
Drake, Dennis	James, Phebe	Feb. 26, 1793
Drummond, Joshua	Kidwell, Mary	March 8, 1786
Drummond, William	Williams, Winny	March 21, 1772
Drummond, Aaron	Oldacres, Nancy	Nov. 3, 1796
Dulin, Lewis	Shud, Ann	Sept. 8, 1789
Dulin, Edward	Rhodes, Elizabeth	Jan. 28, 1788
Dulin, John	Glascock, Fanny	March 24, 1771
Duff, John	Whiting, Mary	Jan. 7, 1788
Duncan, Charles	Kish, Peggy	Nov. 27, 1766
Duncan, Archibald	Williamss, Hannah	August 27, 1792
Duncan, Nimrod	Martin, Hannah	Jan. 11, 1786
Duncan, Joseph	Fletcher, Sarah	Feb. 18, 1766
Duncan, Joseph	Freeman, Hannah	August 21, 1771
Duncan, William	Duncan, Lydia	May 16, 1780
Duncan, Joseph	Jennings, Hannah	Sept. 26, 1785
Duncan, Christopher	Hilburn, Elizabeth	Feb. 15, 1788
Duncan, Benjamin	Foley, Lettice	Sept. 13, 1800
Duncan, Leroy	Williams, Aggy	April 24, 1799
Duncan, Jesse	Duncan, Rose	March 1, 1786
Dye, Martin	Hinson, Hanley	Feb. 3, 1786
Eady, Benjamin	Gillison, Margaret Gibson	March 16, 1787
Eaton, Samuel	McBee, Fanny	Feb. 8, 1791
Edge, Forrester	McCormack, Ann	May 14, 1799

Edge, John, Jr.	Cummins, Mary	Jan. 3, 1781
Einsor, George	Stephens, Docia	Dec. 25, 1785
Edmonds, Elias	Edmonds, Frances	Jan. 11, 1786
Edmonds, William	Foote, Hester	Jan. 12, 1799
Edwards, George W.	Rust, Mary	March 10, 1798
Edwards, Martin	Garner, Celia	March 17, 1783
Edwards, William	Blackwell, Celia	March 16, 1764
Ellis, William	Clendenning, Nancy	Dec. 22, 1789
Ellis, Reuben	Anderson (?), Nancy	Sept. 23, 1805
Elliott, William	Burger, Eleanor	Sept. 22, 1763
Embry, Jesse	Hickerson, Mary	April 4, 1785
Embry, William	Duncan, Franklin	Dec. 22, 1785
Emmons, James	Stigler, Caty	Oct. 14, 1788
Evans, John	Wright, Sary	May, --1800
Evans, Samuel	Mathew, Elpha (?)	March 20, 1793
Evinston, Francis	Corder, Minna	Feb. 18, 1794
Eustace, William	Gillison, Mary	Jan. 21, 1789
Eustace, Isaac	James, Susannah	Dec. 14, 1777
Fannin, John	Riley, Lettice	July 26, 1789
Fant, Armistead	Duff, Ann	July 17, 1798
Farguson, William	Amiss, Dolly	Jan. 25, 1788
Fegan, Edward	Sinkler, Polly	June 22, 1789
Fegan, Daniel	Harrison, Lydia	July 19, 1791
Ferguson, Lewis	Pepper, Holly	Jan. 27, 1783
Ferguson, William	Pepper, Ann	August 28, 1789
Feunce, William	Collins, Lilly	Oct. 22, 1788
Fewell, Benjamin	Henry, Tabitha	June 24, 1795
Fewell, James	Lowe, Mary	Dec. 3, 1794

Fields, Henry	Wheatley, Mary	Feb. 16, 1799
Fields, Thomas	Lawrence, Lydia	Dec. 3, 1793
Fields, Reuben	Jones, Frances	June 1, 1785
Fishback, Jacob	Morgan, Phebe	Feb. 18, 1771
Fisher, Samuel	Pickard, Mary	Dec. 20, 1785
Fletcher, John	Freeman, Elizabeth	May 30, 1780
Fletcher, Richard	Ratcliffe, Elizabeth	Sept. 17, 1788
Fletcher, Benjamin	McKinney, Mary	Sept. 23, 1797
Flinn, William	Stinson, Ann	Jan. 19, 1799
Fleming, Archibald	Watkins, Elizabeth	Jan. 17, 1799
Floweroll (Flowers ?), John	Grigsby, Edith	March 28, 1793
Floweroe (Flowers ?), William	Smith, Ann	August 15, 1799
Floyd, Henry	Crosby, Franky	July 20, 1783
Fitzhugh, Thomas	Moffitt, Charlotte	Feb. 17, 1780
Foley, John	Ashby, Milly	April 24, 1767
Foley, James	Bradford, Mary	March 1, 1789
Foley, James	Ogleby, Elizabeth	August 1, 1785
Fogg, Nathaniel	Giles, Elizabeth	---------
Foard, Thomas	Payne, Molly	Dec. 14, 1799
Ford, George	Calvert (Colvert ?), Charity	Jan. 15,
Ford, Henry	Payne, Nancy	Dec. 16, 1790
Foster, Andrew	Crouch, Jane	August 28, 1789
Foster, William	Bowers, Violet	Nov. 5, 1795
Foster, George	Conway, Sarah	August 25, 1786
Foster, Robert	Leake, Milly	Dec. 25, 1786
Foley, John	Wheatley	August 27, 1787
Foote, William	Foster, Elizabeth	August 26, 1780
Fowkes, Chandler	Harrison, Mary	Dec. 19, 1759

Fox, Charles	Lathane, Elizabeth	July 27, 1799
Frances, Joseph	Holmes, Sebrasta	Sept. 18, 1797
Freeman, William	Settle, Sally	June 15, 1777
Freeman, Harris	---------------	August 21, 1771
Freeman, James	Sharpe, Elizabeth	August 28, 1771
Freeman, James	William, Margaret	March 26, 1782
Froggett, Andrew	Smith, Mooin	August 25, 1788
Frye, Abraham	Morgan, Polly	April 2, 1797
Fulton, James	Downing, Winnifred	Jan. 14, 1799
Furr, John	Furr, Nancy	Jan. 22, 1795
Gabriel, George	Neale, Mary	Oct. 18, 1788
Gant, Ambrose	Vaughn, Sarah	May 26, 1786
Garner, Joseph	Oar (Orr?), Sally	Dec., --1790
Garner, Smith	Balo, Jane	June 22, 1796
Garner, Vincent	Withers, Susannah	April 20, 1799
Garrott, James	Harley, Phebe	----------
Garrott, Nimrod	McCoy, Elizabeth	Feb. 23, 1790
Garrett, James	McKay, Ann	March 13, 1785
George, Aaron	Robinson, Lydia	Oct. 24, 1785
George, Joseph	Shumate, Lydia	June 1, 1786
George, Abner	Thorndyke, Elizabeth	March 18, 1799
George, Reuben	Wilson, Nancy	Nov. 21, 1795
Gibson, Alexander	Jeffries, Lucy	April 28, 1789
Gibson, Robert	Newby, Sinah	Dec. 7, 1790
Gibson, Moses	Wronn, -----	April 7, 1795
Gibson, William	Settle, Hannah	March 31, 1777
Gibson, Thomas	Beale, Charlotte	May 8, 1782

Gibson, John, Jr.	Eustace, Ann	March 24, 1783
Gilbert, Felix	Grant, Ann	Oct. 19, 1761
Gillison, John	Blackwell, Ann Lee	Sept. 10, 1799
Gillison, John	Alexander, Sarah	Sept. 13, 1782
German, Michael (or Gorman)	Masters, Ann	Nov. 6, 1790
Glasscock, Archibald	Kinchloe, Hannah	Oct. 9, 1787
Glasscock, John	Hathaway, Ann	Dec. 1, 1788
Glasscock, Michael	Rector, Catherine	Dec. 2, 1788
Glasscock, William	Green, Ann	Jan. 20, 1789
Gladstone, Arthur	Hitt, Susannah	Dec. 18, 1786
Glendonning (Clendenning ?), Geo.	Duncan, Milly	Jan. 31, 1786
Glascock, Peter	Glascock, Anna	Nov. 24, 1783
Glascock, John	Glascock, Susannah	Jan. 1, 1799
Glascock, Downing	Strother, Sukey	Oct. 30, 1800
Godley, John	Sparks, Elizabeth	March 10, 1796
Goe, Robert	Cox, Allinda	August 2, 1785
Goff, William	Weaver, Frances	Jan. 8, 1790
Golden, Joseph	Henry, Sally	March 16, 1791
Gore, Jonah	Hayes, Parthenia	May 16, 1797
Gough, Bailey	Hensley, Dudley	Oct. 7, 1799
Goulding, Vincent	Burdette, Nancy	March 10, 1790
Graham, George	Blackwell, Alice	June 14, 1785
Gray, Nathaniel	Ransdell, Sally	Sept. 26, 1786
Gray, Thomas	Payne, Patty	Jan. 30, 1792
Gray, Nathaniel	Ransdell, Betsy	March 18, 1789
Grant, Robin	Smith, Sarah	Nov. 22, 1790
Grant, George	Shackleford, Mary	March 12, 1772

Grant, Joseph	Taylor, Elizabeth	Oct. 25, 1796
Grant, William	Clark, Nancy	March 16, 1797
Graves, Duncan	Farrow, Dolly	Sept. 6, 1781
Graves, Thomas	Williams, Amelia	Feb. 9, 1787
Grayer, George	Riley, Elizabeth	Dec. 1, 1788
Green, William	Crockett, Mary Ann	Dec. 18, 1786
Green, Robert	Edmonds, Frances	August 15, 1787
Green, James	Triplett, Celia	Feb. 18, 1787
Green, William	Blackwell, Lucy	May 13, 1775
Green, James	Jones, Elizabeth	Jan. 28, 1782
Green, Gabriel	Grant, Sarah Ann	Sept. 23, 1783
Green, John	Collins, Betsy	May 12, 1785
Green, Moses	Blackwell, Mary	Feb. 13, 1764
Green, George	Barnes, Dinah	May 23, 1799
Greenwood, Henry	Dye, Sarah	July 23, 1799
Grigsby, William	Bullitt, Elizabeth	Feb. 8, 1771
Grigsby, Aaron	Moffitt, Milly	Jan. 28, 1785
Grigsby, Taliaferro	Keith, Elizabeth	Feb. 15, 1785
Grigsby, Benjamin	Duncan, Elizabeth	Dec. 23, 1786
Grigsby, Samuel	Cornwell, Franky	Sept. 4, 1786
Grigsby, Benjamin	Browning, Alice	---24, 1790
Griffin, George	Glascock, Molly	Dec. 24, 1787
Grimsley, Nimrod	Roberts, Amelia	Dec. 17, 1787
Groves, John	Crump, Sarah	May 7, 1790
Gutridge, Reuben	Payne, Susannah	Jan. 7, 1794
Gutridge, Peter	Chadwell, Lucy	Nov. 11, 1794
Gutridge, Allen	Deal, Lucy	Dec. 15, 1790

92

Hackley, James	Freeman, Mary	June 14, 1771
Haddux, Abraham	Hefflin, Ann	Jan. 26, 1795
Hagan, John	Mauzy, Molly	Oct. 31, 1781
Hailey, Anthony	Dennison, Mary	Sept. 20, 1785
Hailey, John	Jett, Peggy	Sept. 19, 1785
Hailey, William	Jett, Nancy	Dec. 23, 1786
Heinor, George	Whitley, Selah	May 18, 1799
Hailey, William	Jett, Susan	Sept. 16, 1790
Hall, John	Monroe, Sarah	May 13, 1791
Hall, William	Kennard, Frances	May 29, 1789
Hammons, John	Hefferling, Susannah	July 20, 1788
Hampton, George	Ballard, Mary Nugent	Nov. 14, 1782
Hampton, William	Hinton, Fanny	Dec. 14, 1773
Hampton, Thomas	Morehead, Lucy	Sept. 2, 1794
Hampton, Joseph	Hathaway, Margaret	April 9, 1787
Hamrick, Gilson	Thomas, Sally	Nov. 9, 1785
Hand, John	Robinson, Jenny Arglo	--- No date
Haney, Thomas	Chappelle, Margaret	Dec. 26, 1789
Hansborough, John	Shehogan, Sarah	March 3, 1789
Hansborough, William	Watts, Sarah	April 27, 1766
Hansborough, Peter	Harrison, Ann	Oct. 23, 1790
Harley, Joseph	Hummins (Cummins?), Sally	Oct. 26, 1797
Harrill, ----	Shanks, Katy	Dec. 31, 1787
Harris, George	Harris, Catherine	June 16, 1773
Hancock, William	Grigsby, Susannah	Oct. 27, 1788
Harrington, John	Shank, Susannah	April 26, 1791
Harris, Elisha	McCormack, Margaret	Nov. 21, 1780
Harris, Samuel	Duncan, Nancy	August 23, 1789

Harris, Arthur	Toff, Elizabeth	Sept. 3, 1785
Harris, Henry	Williams, Joanna	Oct. 15, 1787
Harrison, Burr	Pickett, Lucy	Aug. 24, 1789
Hardin, Benjamin	Routt, Nancy	March 16, 1785
Harrison, William	Humston, Jane	Feb. 23, 1767
Harper, Isaac	Constable, Jemima	April 15, 1787
Haugh, James	Barratt, Nancy	Nov. 25, 1795
Hathaway, James	Nevill, Joanna	March 25, 1771
Hatfield, Stewart	Fidler, Rebecca	Sept. 6, 1788
Hawkins, Jesse	Jones, Polly	March 8, 1797
Hawkins, Benjamin	Bowers, Ann	October 29, 1764
Hayes, Jacob	Rector, Betty	Dec. 21, 1785
Hayne, Jonathan	Whitacre, Martha	Feb. 5, 1795
Head, Richard	Newport, Sarah	Jan. 5, 1771
Head, Cornelius	Hilkins, Margaret	Jun. 14, 1790
Headley, Robert	Boley, Elisabeth	March 9, 1797
Headley, James	Jeffries, Lucy	June 14, 1783
Heaton, Thomas	Taylor, Susannah	March 11, 1789
Heaton, James	Harris, Martha	Dec. 2, 1797
Hefflin, William	Collins, Lilly	Oct. 27, 1789
Helm, William	Pickett, Agatha	March 3, 1789
Helm, William	Neaville, Lettice	Feb. 23, 1764
Henderson, Pierce Bayley	Duncan, Milly	Dec. 17, 1789
Herndon, George	Stephen, Elisabeth	Sept. 1, 1790
Hickman, John	Thompson, Ann	June 20, 1790
Hickman, John	Thompson, Ann	July 1, 1790
Hickman, William	Rakestraw, Nancy	April 9, 1796

Higgison, Walter	Elley, Esther	Nov. 23, 1793
Hill, James	Leach, Sarah	Feb. 19, 1788
Hinson, Dennis	Doty, Elizabeth	March 23, 1796
Hinson, James	Cushenberry (Quisenberry), Ann	Jan. 18,
Hinson, George	Little, Susannah	Sept. 17, 1771
Hinson, Jesse	Sullivan, Mary	April 19, 1787
Hinson, Jesse	Crawford, Eliz.	Nov. 28, 1787
Hitch, Wise	Williams, Nancy	Sept. 24, 1797
Hitch, John	Elgin, Casandra	Feb. 27, 1787
Hitt, John	Holtzclaw, Franky	Nov. 25, 1793
Hitt, Peter	Hitt, Lucy	August 23, 1796
Hogan, Rawleigh	Conway, Peggy	May 21, 1786
Holder, Dorris	Shumate, Anna	July 11, 1786
Holtzclaw, Archibald	Hitt, Miriam	Jan. 3, 1786
Holtzclaw, Nathaniel	Gibson, Isa	April 8, 1782
Holtzclaw, Amos	Hopwood, Sally	Oct. 7, 1799
Holly, Rolly	Calvin, Mary	Dec. 20, 1788
Homes, Edwin	Starke, Sarah Ann	April 23, 1764
Hoomes, Nathaniel	Jones, Betty	Oct. 17, 1799
Homes, James	Hume, Agatha	Jan. 11, 1786
Hopp, Thomas	Bird, Mary	August 21, 1796
Hopper, John	McMookin, ---	Feb. 12, 1782
Hopper, William	Williams, Litty	Feb. 9, 1788
Hord, James	Hord, Sarah	March 11, 1786
Hord, Peter	Wheatley, Honor	May 28, 1771
Horner, William	Edmond, Mary	Oct. 19, 1790
Horner, Gustavus Brown	Scott, Frances	April 13, 1785
Horton, Charles	Cooper, Elisabeth	Dec. 29, 1788

Horton, Elijah	Nelson, Catherine	Feb. 12, 1781
Horton, Craven	Newhouse, Polly	Feb. 8, 1799
Hotten, William	Cook, Betty	Nov. 3, 1795
Howell, Benjamin	Harper, Sally	Nov. 23, 1795
Hubbard, Ephiram	Edmonds, Ann	Dec. 27, 1773
Hubbard, Epaphroditus	Edmonson, Ann McCarthy	Oct. 20, 1785
Hudnall, William	Cockrell, Roannah	Feb. 20, 1793
Hudnall, Joseph	Taylor, Mary	Nov. 30, 1759
Huffman, William	Guy, Ann	April 29, 1789
Hughes, Abraham	Marshall, Sarah	Feb. 20, 1780
Humes, Charles	James, Hannah	Dec. 26, 1764
Humston, Edward	Quarles, Susannah	Jan. 13, 1768
Humphrie, John	McConchie, Dorothy	April 21, 1790
Hurley, Daniel	Riley, Nancy	Dec. 23, 1791
Ingram, Thomas	Brooks, Lucy	Nov. 21, 1799
Ireland, James	Burgess, Jane	April 16, 1771
Jacobs William	Boswell, Mary	June 18, 1789
Jackson, Samuel	Grinnan, Vashti	August 11, 1771
Jackson, Dempsey	Pickett, Molly	Dec. 29, 1787
Jackson, Daniel	Tolls, Anne	July 3, 1793
Jackman, Richard	Neavill, Mary	May 2, 1766
Jackson, Samuel	Jackson, Peggy	Feb. 9, 1799
Jackson, Ephiram	Norman, Tabitha	Sept. 9, 1799
James, Benjamin	----- Elizabeth	May 14, 1799
James, Isaac	Parker, Sarah	Jan. 3, 1787
James, John	Wood, Louisa	Jan. 8, 1787
James, John	Wright, Elizabeth	June 27, 1785
James, Joseph	James, Mary	June 3, 1777

James, Thomas	White, Hannah	Dec. 11, 1787
Jeffries, Ephiram	Norman, Tabitha	Sept. 9, 1799
Jeffries, Joseph	Young, Mary	Sept. 12, 1785
Jeffries, John	Coodnick, Alice	March 27, 1786
Jeffries, Henry	Chumberlain, Margaret	Aug. 18, 1788
Jeffries, Anderson	Goodin, Mary	Aug. 18, 1788
Jeffries, Briant	Dulin, Mary	Jan. 19, 1799
Jeffries, Thomas	Hume, Frances	Sept. 24, 1795
Jenkins, John	Shaver, Rebecca	June 2, 1792
Jenkins, Thomas	Robinson, Katy	Nov. 1, 1786
Jennings, Alexander	Bronbaugh, Nancy	May 19, 1799
Jennings, Lewis	Bradford, Lucinda	Oct. 4, 1786
Jennings, William	Withers, Elizabeth	Dec. 24, 1764
Jermert, Joshua	Wright, Mary	Feb. 8, 1797
Jett, James	Grant, Aggy	Dec. 29, 1795
John, Benjamin	Stevenson, (?), Patty	March 13, 1798
Johnson, Archibald	Obanon, Jemina	Nov. 30, 1786
Johnson, Bushby	Welch, Margaret	Sept. 1, 1791
Johnson, Charles	Barber, Nancy	Nov. 14, 1797
Johnson, David	Odor, Sarah	March 21, 1789
Johnson, Minor	Johnson, Hannah	Feb. 23, 1790
Johnson, Nimrod	Adams, Polly	Feb. 24, 1790
Johnson, Tennis	Settle, Rose	Aug. 8, 1788
Johnson, Thomas	Miller, Molly	Sept. 3, 1795
Johnson, John	Crockell, Sally	Jan. 5, 1797
Johnson, Wilfred	Peyton, Mary	Aug. 21, 1786
Jones, Levi	Smoot, Franky	Jan. 31, 1799

Jones, Robert	Ashby, Dolly	June 23, 1789
Jones, Edward	Hathaway, Eliz.	June 21, 1790
Jones, Isaiah	Thomas, Susannah	Dec. 3, 1795
Jones, Moses	Hamilton, Sarah	Feb. 4, 1786
Jones, Richard	Guy, Sarah	April 19, 1786
Jones, John	Weeks, Peggy	Sept. 28, 1794
Jones, John	Murphy, Jane	--- 18, 1797
Jones, Joseph	Brooks, Molly	Jan. 2, 1794
Jones, John Warner	Tullos, Mary	Sept. 29, 1788
Jones, James	Bradford, Mary	Dec. 21, 1786
Jones, John	Tibbetts, Elizabeth	Dec. 30, 1786
Jones, Robert	Florence, Hannah	No date-----
Jones, William	Eustace, Ann	Dec. 14, 1780
Kampe, Peter	Fisher, Susannah	Oct. 18, 1788
Kamper, Frederick	Jeffries, Molly	Oct. 24, 1773
Keith, Thomas	Blackwell, Judith	May 23, 1775
Kemper, Lewis	Bayse, Hannah	Jan. 26, 1789
Kempor, John	Fisher, Martha	May 2, 1787
Kemper, Martin	Kemper, Rosanna	July 3, 1799
Kemper, Thomas	Kemper, Anna	August 21, 1799
Kemper, David	Kemper, Nancy	--------
Kendall, Jesse	Easthane, Catherine	Jan. 16, 1781
Kenner, Robert	Clark, Dolly	Feb. 11, 1785
Kenner, Rodham	Barker, Jemina	Nov. 26, 1787
Kenny, Andrew	Horton, Nancy	Dec. 23, 1789
Korns, Thomas	Russell, Mary	August 26, 1786
Korns, Jacob	Roboy (or Roley), Betsy	Jan. 17, 1799
Koy, Thomas	Foley, Sarah	June 29, 1793

Key, Price	Queens, Sally	March 25, 1787
Kibble (or Kebble), William	Kebble, Mary	Dec. 17, 1799
Kidwell, Thomas	Pearson, Elizabeth	April 5, 1788
Kinchloe, James	Hardewicke, Elizabeth	Dec. 7, 1790
King, John	Bethel, Ann	Nov. 23, 1790
King, Joshua	Kennaday, Rachel	Nov. 24, 1780
King, George	Johnston, Elizabeth	July 12, 1795
Kirby, James	Campbell, Nancy	Aug. 7, 1790
Kirkpatrck, William	Fegan, Mary	Nov. 23, 1786
Kittson, John	Brown, Mary	Dec. 5, 1787
Knight, John	Boscarver, Susanna	July 4, 1787
Knowlong (Knowland), John	Arnold, Jemina	Oct. 12, 1785
Lacy, Nathaniel	Grant, Mary	Sept. 11, 1793
Lacy, Moses	Pratt, Henrietta	March 3, 1787
Lake, Vincent	Drummond, Frances	Jan. 16, 1793
Lamkin, James	Barker, Sarah	Sept. 24, 1786
Lanketer, Alexander	Vanderbilt, Chloe	Feb. 22, 1794
Larrance, John	Obannon, Joyce	March 13, 1786
Lawerence, Edward	Priest, Nancy	Jan. 29, 1786
Laworence, Mason	Obannon, Nancy	March 24, 1788
Laworence, Rodham	Lawerence, Eliz.	Jan. 9, 1786
Leach, J ----	Hall, Molly	Oct. 4, 1796
Leach, George	Craig, Ann	July 16, 1785
Leach, George	Bigbie, ----	Dec. 27, 1785
Leach, Valentine	Furrow, Molly	June 23, 1785
Leach, Marshall	Davidson, Ann	Aug. 28, 1793
Leake, Bazie	Anderson, Mary	Jan. 22, 1795

Lear (Sear), William	Bailey, Hannah	Aug. 8, 1786
Lee, Hancock	Hancock, Lena Ann	Aug. 23, 1788
Lee, James	Lee, Mary	Feb. 2, 1787
Lewis, Jacob	Lewis, Lovey	June 10, 1793
Lewis, Britain	Crump, Ann	March 3, 1788
Linn, Joseph	Brooke, Sarah	Dec. 8, 1789
Linn, Alexander	Kamper, Hannah	Oct. 28, 1782
Little, Jordan	Crafford, Lucy	Feb. 15, 1786
Lion, John	Holtzclaw, Susannah	June 18, 1787
Lloyd, George Emory	Brown, Ann	July 3, 1787
Lloyd, Joseph	Brown, Frances	Oct. 4, 1797
Logan, John	Gibson, Alse	Dec. 11, 1797
Logan, Henry	Herring, Catherine	June 27, 1789
Lowe, John	Adams, Franky	March 2, 1789
Lowe, Jesse	Kemper, Fanny	Nov. 29, 1798
Lowry, Daniel	Emory, Ann	April 26, 1786
Lowry, William	Grant, Elizabeth	Jan. 22, 1799
Love, William	McClanahan, Lettice	Dec. 24, 1795
Lunsford, John	Fowkes, Elizabeth	Jan. 8, 1787
Lunsford, Rodham	Ball, Clementine	Dec. 18, 1786
Lunsford, Roldy	Crocs, Judith	Dec. 26, 1796
Luttrell, Nelson	Tharpe, Fanny	Sept. 1, 1802
Luttrell, John	Smith, Hannah	April 2, 1791
Lynn, Francis	Wheatley, Sarah	Jan. 22, 1799
Mackarel, James	Morgan, Sally	April 26, 1790
Maddux, Jesse	Blackorby, Judith	June 8, 1782
Maddux, Nathaniel	Tonnison, Ann	March 9, 1786

Maddux, George	Neale, Judith	Jan. 21, 1795
Mahoney, Benjamin	Harris, Elizabeth	Dec. 21, 1785
Mahoney, Misten (or Martin)	Smith, Jemima	Dec. 22, 1795
Majors, Alexander	Howell, Lotty	Dec. 24, 1787
Mallory, James	Dowell, Elizabeth	Sept. 6, 1792
Mallory, Philip	Harrison, Jane	Nov. 24, 1783
Mallory, William	Harrison, Lucy	Jan. 12, 1785
Markham, William	Smith, Mary	July 28, 1789
Markham, James	Konner, Catherine	Nov. 20, 1770
Marshall, Simon	---- Caty	Oct. 22, 1794
Marshall, Thomas, Jr.	Adams, Susannah	Sept. 11, 1783
Marshall, John	Benn, Rachel	Jan. 22, 1790
Marshall, Charles	Pickett, Lucy	Sept. 11, 1787
Martin, Charles	Stigler, Martha	Sept. 1, 1791
Martin, James	Hughes, Agatha	April 17, 1789
Martin, Charles	Fishback, Franky	Aug. 9, 1790
Martin, Nimrod	Hopwood, Fanny	Dec. 22, 1787
Martin, George	McCormack, Eliz.	Oct. 24, 1785
Mason, Jesse	Embry, Nancy	Feb. 12, 1788
Mason, Thomas	Singleton, Caty	May 15, 1790
Mason, Colbert	Rogers, Margaret	March 25, 1786
Massey, Thomas	Morehead, Molly	Dec. 23, 1772
Mathers, Robert	Rogers, Sally	Jan. 10, 1787
Mathews, Simon	Stamps, Molly	Dec. 26, 1788
Mather, Benjamin	Snyder, Mary	May 18, 1795
Mauzy, Henry	Morgan, Elizabeth	July 23, 1764
Mauzy, Peter	Shumate, Sarah	Dec. 4, 1799
Maybin, David	Konner, Catherine	Dec. 15, 1785

101

Mayes, Henry	Palmer, Mary	Dec. 26, 1796
Metalfe, Asa	Weeks, Elizabeth	July 24, 1796
Metcalfe, Charles	Blackerby, Elizabeth	Jan. 18, 1781
Metcalfe, John	Shackleford, Milly	May 1, 1782
Metcalfe, Elias	Pickett, Sally	Dec. 29, 1788
Meall, Samuel	Luttrell, Elizabeth	Dec. 26, 1788
Middleton, Studley	Wickliffe, Nancy	Oct. 29, 1788
Miller, John	Mitt, Nancy	Dec. 16, 1789
Miller, Henry	Neale, Lettice	Feb. 10, 1791
Minor, George	Heale, Mildred	Jan. 22, 1788
Mitchell, John	Rosser, Mary	Dec. 21, 1771
Mitchell, Joshua	Stiggens, Elizabeth	Dec. 22, 1788
Moffett, William	Stone, Ann	Feb. 3, 1760
Monday, Charles	Fishback, Polly	Dec. 13, 1793
Mourse, George	Green, Mary	Sept. 26, 1786
Monroe, James	Willis, Sally	Jan. 25, 1787
Moore, McLanahan	Metcalfe, Eliz.	Nov. 21, 1786
Morehead, George	Hampton, Sally	Jan. 5, 1791
Morehead, Charles	Slaughter, Margaret	Oct. 30, 1786
Morgan, Benjamin	Kenner, Elizabeth	Oct. 31, 1782
Morgan, C.	Glascock, Margaret	Jan. 15, 1790
Morgan, Francis	Read, Mary	Nov. 20, 1773
Morgan, Charles	Robinson, Mary	Jan. 1, 1781
Morgan, Joseph	Bradford, Elizabeth	Nov. 26, 1773
Morgan, Spencer	Kenner, Susannah	Oct. 14, 1780
Morgan, John	Thomas, Anne	Oct. 12, 1782
Moring, John	Fishback, Sarah	June 12, 1790
Moore, Francis	Foote, Frances	April 2, 1764

Moore, Samuel	Payne, Lucy	May 1, 1782
Moore, Samuel	McFeavor, Elizabeth	Nov. 22, 1768
Moore, Samuel	Hill, Sarah (widow)	Nov. 11, 1799
Morris, David	McDonald, Lydia	Dec. 20, 1793
Morrison, John	Berditt, Peggy	Sept. 24, 1793
Moss, William	Glascock, Lydia	Sept. 13, 1786
Moss, Tealy	Glascock, Jenny	Sept. 13, 1786
Moss, Daniel	Hathaway, Sarafta	March 3, 1795
Mott, William	Welch, Mary	August 22, 1785
Murray, Enoch	Crosby, Frances	August 7, 1787
Murry, Benjamin	Grant, Elizabeth	March 14, 1787
Murry, Reuben	Chinn, Catherine	Sept. 24, 1795
Murphy, David	Roe, Lydia	Dec. 27, 1797
Murphy, Leander	Duncan, Rose	Feb. 11, 1789
Murphy, William	Bowen, Sally	Dec. 16, 1790
Murchow, John	Waddell, Jane	Sept. 24, 1781
Myers, Michael	Thornberry, Margaret	April 2, 1774
McBee, John	Randall, Margaret	Dec. 22, 1790
Mc Bee, Benjamin	Randall, Hannah	Jan. 28, 1789
McCaron, Daniel	Dodd, Mary	Oct. 29, 1789
McCarty, (?) Cornelius	Hardwicke, Sukey	Dec. 12, 1787
McClanahan, John	Elliott, Sally	Nov. 5, 1795
McClanahan, William	Tolling, Elizabeth	Nov. 23, 1789
McClanahan, Gerrard	Rust, Sally	May 5, 1796
McClanahan, David	Frye, Elizabeth	June 3, 1786
McCloud, Martin	Fowkes, Nancy	Nov. 15, 1790
McCoy, Joseph	Williams, Mary	March 15, 1787
Mc Coy, Daniel	Kemper, Agnes	Feb. 10, 1790

McConchi, Robert	King, Mary Ann	Dec. 25, 1790
McDaniel, John	Oliman (Climan) Ann	Dec. 15, 1788
McDaniel, John	Horton, Finton	June 19, 1786
McDonald, Archibald	Lowry, Mary	March 21, 1790
McDonald, Jared	Marshall, Nancy	Jan. 25, 1795
McEntree, William	Glascock, Phebe	Jan. 28, 1799
McGraw, Isaiah	Morris, Anne	Oct. 19, 1797
McKonny, Mathew	Milton, Mary	Dec. 31, 1796
McMocker, Archibald	Johnson, Margaret	Feb. 27, 1800
McNeal, William	Kearne, Elizabeth	August 24, 1790
Nalls, William	Blithe, Mary	Dec. 28, 1796
Nash, William	Bradford, Mary	Feb. 23, 1764
Nay, Joseph	Mahoney, Frances	Jan. 10, 1789
Neale, Thomas	Rozier, Elizabeth	April 14, 1790
Neale, James	Pinckard, Sarah	Dec. 18, 1788
Neavil, Joseph	Ellott, Mary	Dec. 20, 1777
Neavil, Thomas	Stewart, Mary	July 31, 1772
Nelson, Joseph	Obannon, Catherine	Dec. 23, 1771
Nelson, John	Withers, Seathley	Sept. 14, 1796
Nelson, Joseph	Bradford, Jane	April 18, 1790
Nelson, James	Obannon, Betty	Feb. 11, 1765
Nelson, John	Hegain, Bathasheba	Dec. 10, 1780
Nelson, Thomas	Grigsby, Rachel	Oct. 24, 1768
Nowland, William	Turner, Nancy	Oct. 7, 1799
Norman, George	Utterback, Elisabeth	Jan. 22, 1799
Norris, Septimus	Brown, Margaret	Nov. 5, 1795
Norris, John	Jones, Mary	March 25, 1782
Northcutt, John	Henry, Nancy	Jan. 1, 1789

Northcutt, Benjamin	Brooks, Winny	Dec. 19, 1788
Nutt, Richard	Hathaway, Eliza	Nov. 26, 1788
Obannon, Andrew	Smith, Mary (widow)	Oct. 10, 1777
Obannon, Benjamin	Ash, Eleanor	Nov. 13, 1780
Obannon, Joseph	Grigsby, Elizabeth	Sept. 2, 1782
Obannon, Thomas	Barker, Hannah	Jan. 21, 1783
Oliver, Josias	Morehead, Mary	August 28, 1789
Oliver, Samuel	Brown, Elizabeth	April 24, 1787
Oneal, Thomas	Murray, Esther	April 24, 1787
Orear, Jesse	Holton, Malinda	Dec. 20, 1783
Owens, Aaron	Hathaway, Dorothy	Oct. 1, 1794
Owens, Bethel	Owens, Elizabeth	Dec. 17, 1787
Owens, Mason	Flourence, Sarah	Nov. 13, 1796
Owens, Thomas	Austin, Nancy	Dec. 30, 1786
Owens, William	Owens, Nancy	Nov. 27, 1786
Paine, William	Johnston, Nelly	May 27, 1796
Parker, Joseph	Duncan, Betty	Jan. 11, 1781
Parker, Abraham	McKay, Priscilla	Feb. 18, 1789
Parker, Martin	Shumate, Mary	Dec. 24, 1787
Parker, Thomas	Marshall, Alice	Nov. 23, 1793
Parmer, Isaac	Tomson, Milly	Nov. 15, 1792
Parsons, William	Holtzclaw, Eliz.	Jan. 4, 1797
Patterson, James	Constable, Nancy	Nov. 3, 1790
Paulie, Issachar	Bryan, Rachel	Nov. 15, 1783
Payne, Augustine	Young, Caty	Jan. 14, 1789
Payne, Benjamin	Rosseau, Susannah	Jan. 2, 1781
Payne, Coldton	Smoot, Charity	Oct. 20, 1790
Payne Merryman	Johnson, Frances	March 17, 1789

Payne, William, Jr.	Payne, Molly	March 17, 1789
Peach, John	Neale, Nancy	Jan. 4, 1800
Pearle, Samuel	Strother, Nancy	June 15, 1790
Pearle, Samuel	Kerr, Dorcas	Aug. 25, 1773
Pearle, Samuel	Darnale, Delia	March 26, 1798
Pearle, William	Thompson, Ann	July 1, 1790
Pendleton, Robert	Haddrick, Charlotte	Dec. 30, 1792
Penny, James	Dulin, Lydia	May 30, 1789
Pepper, Elijah	Obannon, Sally	Feb. 20, 1793
Pepper, Jesse	Lamkin, Betty	Feb. 2, 1796
Pepper, Jeremiah	Billingsby, Ellander	July 6, 1797
Peters, James	Starke, Sally	Feb. 8, 1796
Peters, James	Ashby, Winnifred	Jan. 17, 1764
Peters, John	Rousann, Ann	Oct. 20, 1783
Petty, Marshall	Bowmer, Jemina	Dec. 15, 1794
Pettot, Nathaniel	Owen, Rebecca	Oct. 19, 1781
Pettot, Samuel	Bragg, Elizabeth	Dec. 10, 1783
Pettot, Thomas	Owen, Betholen	April 16, 1785
Peyton, Valentine	Halo, Sally	Dec. 21, 1789
Peyton, Cuthbert	Brough, Catherine	May 26, 1782
Phillips, Fielding	Linton, Nancy	Feb. 5, 1799
Phillips, William	Fowkes, Elizabeth	June 7, 1774
Pollard, Abner	Clark, Harriet	Jan. 18, 1798
Pope, Benjamin	Young, Mary	Jan. 15, 1766
Popkins, John	Perry, Sally	Nov. 6, 1787
Porter, Eppa	Porter, Elizabeth	Oct. 17, 1799
Porter, Eli	Halo, Martha	Jan. 5, 1800

Porter, Thomas	Porter, Susannah	Dec. 31, 1782
Porter, Charles	Bonson, Ann	March 11, 1786
Porter, John	Smith, Jean	June 7, 1785
Porter, Martin	Withers, Aggy	March 16, 1789
Porter, Samuel	------Polly	August 22, 1796
Porter, Edwin	Mauzy, Polly	Sept. 25, 1797
Porter, Christopher	Baker, Elizabeth	March 17, 1789
Powell, Henry	Strothers, Sally	April 9, 1787
Powers, Patrick	Snyder, Caty	Oct. 12, 1790
Powers, Thomas	Fields, Elizabeth	Sept. 12, 1793
Powan (or Rowan), William	Griffin, Mary	Dec. 26, 1796
Pickett, John	Chamberlain, Eliz.	Nov. 20, 1790
Pickett, Martin	Blackwell, Ann	May 31, 1764
Pickett, William Sanford	Smith, Martha	Sept. 26, 1795
Pierce, John	Hume, Patience	June 4, 1793
Pilcher, Steven	Fishback, Sarah	Jan. 9, 1793
Pilcher, William	Fishback, Lilly Tibbs	April 26, 1797
Pratt, Zephania	Cooke, Ann	April 22, 1782
Prago, John	Kirke, Elizabeth	July 20, 1781
Priest, Mason	Lawrence, Sally	Jan. 20, 1786
Prainer, Philip	Wolf, Catherine	Dec. 8, 1796
Price, Richard	James, Peggy	August 3, 1776
Price, Samuel	Clemans, Mary	March 23, 1793
Brumm (or Brimm), John	Simmons, Catherine	--- No date--
Brimm, Thomas	Johnson, Sally	July 30, 1795
Race, William	Senton, Jenny	May 12, 1796
Ralls, Charles	Brown, Hannah	Aug. 24, 1780
Ralls, Joel	Bird, Lona	June 23, 1796

Ransdell, Thomas	Ransdell, Mary	Nov. 8, 1786
Ransdell, Wharton	Morehead, Mary	Jan. 16, 1781
Read, Thomas	Fishback, Milly	April 25, 1785
Read, Theophielus	Duncan, Peggy	Nov. 16, 1797
Rector, Moses	Green, Elizabeth	Feb. 25, 1788
Rector, Spencer	Tiffin, Mary	Oct. 3, 1785
Rector, Lewis	Green, Elizabeth	Dec. 22, 1794
Redd, Allen	Bullitt, Elizabeth	July 28, 1777
Renas (or Rence), Zeky	Chinn, Mary	July 26, 1775
Resen, Thomas	Kennady, Sarah	Dec. 2, 1800
Rence, George	Baylis, Joan	Feb. 20, 1785
Rhodes, John	Doubtman, Nancy	Nov. 10, 1768
Rhodes, Hezekiah	Putman, Elizabeth	Jan. 20, 1765
Rhodes, Jacob	Green, Frances	Oct. 5, 1792
Rickett, James	Smith, Nancy	June 5, 1800
Rickard, William	Blackwell, Ann	Feb. 21, 1786
Rice, Bailey	Morehead, Eliz.	June 19, 1789
Ridley, John	Bailey, Elizabeth	April 24, 1781
Rodding, Reuben	Robert, Elizabeth	Jan. 26, 1789
Rings, (or Ringo), Burtis	Rector, Hannah	Feb. 22, 1790
Rixby, Richard, Jr.	Morehead, Eliz.	Nov. 18, 1764
Roach, John	McClanahan, Patty	August 24, 1785
Roach, George	White, Sarah	August 25, 1789
Robertson, Benjamin	James, Margaret Bruce	Oct. 31, 1783
Robinson, William	Lee, Susannah	March 13, 1790
Robertson, John	Benson, Elizabeth	Sept. 8, 1787
Robinson, Elijah	Norris, Susannah	Oct. 3, 1785

Robinson, James	Robinson, Molly	Jan. 23, 1790
Robert, John	Holly, Sally	June 22, 1789
Robinson, George	Foster, Ann	Aug. 25, 1789
Robinson, William	Garner, Nancy	March 28, 1796
Robinson, David	Wilson, Sally	April 5, 1790
Robinson, Maxmillian	Elliott, Jemina	Jan. 27, 1796
Robinson, Dixon	Pinkstone, Anna	Feb. 2, 1793
Roe, Steven	Clendenning, Peggy	Oct. 23, 1799
Roger, Henry	Jett, Sally	March 23, 1789
Roe, William	Glascock, Toally	Dec. 20, 1792
Roose, Nicholas	Hichlhorn, Eve	Dec. 12, 1799
Rossen, John	Clendenning, Molly	Feb. 22, 1781
Routte, Daniel	Stegler (Stigler), Martha	Sept. 6, 1788
Roose, Aaron	Phillips, Ruth	March 26, 1786
Roe, Original	Konnor, Sarah	June 16, 1788
Rouins, James	Finch, Polly	Oct. 31, 1799
Roy, Willy	Fowkes, Sarah	Dec. 26, 1772
Routt, Peter	Crosby, Ann	June 6, 1765
R ---, Richard	Morehead, Polly	Dec. 31, 1775
Runnells, John	Phillips, Caty	Oct. 30, 1794
Russell, Daniel	Matthew, Rachel	August 15, 1792
Russell, William	Darnall, Mary	Oct. 18, 1771
Rusley, George	Jeffries, Mary	April 29, 1797
Rust, John	Atkinson, Elenn	Jan. 20, 1771
Rust, Peter	Taylor, Eliza	Dec. 3, 1799
Rust, John	McClanahan, Molly	Dec. 28, 1796
Russell, William	Curtis, Mary	Jan. 12, 1787

Sanders, Thomas	Rogers, Molly	June 1, 1785
Saunders, William	Jeffries, Agnes	Jan. 15, 1790
Santland, Fielding	Spiller, (?), Sophia	April 23, 1786
Scott, Charles	Stanton, Lucinda	Oct. 8, 1798
Scott, William	Sullivan, Mary Ann	--------1790
Seaton, George	Seaton, Sarah	May 23, 1786
Seaton, John	Murry, Alice	Oct. 21, 1768
Seaton, William	Kenner, Mary	Feb. 6, 1764
Selman (or Silman), Zack	Lawerence, Janney	August 7, 1790
Settle, Edward	Morgan, Rosanna	Sept. 28, 1772
Settle, Strother	Ash, Dorothy	June 10, 1782
Settle, William	Gavner, Sally	June 13, 1786
Settle, William	Hunton, Melinda	May 11, 1787
Sharpe, Spencer	Arnold, Nancy	April 15, 1793
Shaw, Charles	Jett, Catherine	Jan. 19, 1790
Shaw, John	Cleveland, Fanny	July 10, 1785
Shaver, John	Neale, Mary	Feb. 17, 1789
Shults, Joseph	Thompson, Sally	Dec. 15, 1794
Shesterson, George	Baker, Lettice	April 17, 1792
Shipp, Laban	Turner, Rebecca	Feb. 10, 1786
Shipp, Elijah	Price, Rebecca	Jan. 10, 1792
Shipp, Joseph	Etcheson, Letty	Oct. 2, 1785
Shirley, James	McMookin, Mary	Oct. 9, 1781
Short, John	Leach, Nancy	Dec. 25, 1794
Shumate, Benjamin	Gregory, Winny	March 31, 1790
Shumate, Hohn	Preston, Sarah	Jan. 28, 1788
Shumato, John	Crump, Susannah	Sept. 2, 1775
Shumato, William	Morman, Frances	Feb. 26, 1787

Shurlock, James	Norman, Judy	Sept. 20, 1785
Slaughter, Cadwalder	Fowkes, Mary	August 4, 1786
Slaughter, Henry	Taylor, Romey	Sept. 26, 1786
Slaughter, Jess	Hampton, Elizabeth	July 22, 1772
Slaughter, Joseph	Harper, Rachel	Feb. 5, 1787
Slaughter, Matthew	Thomas, Ann	Dec. 18, 1798
Slaughter, Samuel	Lampkin, Peggy	Dec. 14, 1798
Slaughter, Samuel	Jenkins, Peggy	Dec. 15, 1798
Smarr, Andrew	Murray, Lydia	Dec. 8, 1791
Smedley, William	Simpson, Lydia	Apl. 17, 1791
Smith, Augustine	Chilton, Nancy	Dec. 15, 1798
Smith, Augustine	Darnall, Susannah	Dec. 30, 1780
Smith, Berryman	Martin, Elizabeth	August 31, 1785
Smith, Caleb	Smith, Mary Waugh	Dec. 18, 1794
Smith, Delaney	Wright, Mary	Sept. 26, 1785
Smith, James	Pickett, Sebba	June 16, 1796
Smith, James	Bencor, Clacy	Dec. 16, 1798
Smith, John	Dodd, Elizabeth	Dec. 19, 1796
Smith, John	Spicer, Rebecca	Dec. 24, 1787
Smith, Matthew	Winn, Martha	April 25, 1771
Smith, John	Berryman, Mary	April 22, 1777
Smith, John	Allen, Margaret	Oct. 24, 1788
Smith, John	Williams, Betty	April 14, 1789
Smith, Lewis	Davis, Ruth	April 21, 1798
Smith, Scarlett	Jackson, Lydia	March 19, 1788
Smith, Thomas	Adams, Elizabeth	June 26, 1769
Smith, William	Ashly, Ann	April 18, 1782
Smith, William	McQueen, Elizabeth	July 23, 1789

Smoot, Claiborne	Payne, Mary	Feb. 4, 1790
Smoot, Edward	Hitch, Susannah	June 11, 1788
Smoot, John	Hitch (Hatch), Peggy	Dec. 16, 1789
Smoot, Lewis	Marvet (or Marvel), Eliz.	Feb. 8, 1799
Snyder, Nimrod	Hall, Catherine	Nov. 28, 1795
Snape, Nathaniel	Kidwell, Fanny	Dec. 20, 1789
Sparks, James	Dawson, Margaret	Dec. 15, 1785
Spellman, John	Freeman, Elizabeth	Jan. 1, 1797
Spettler (?), Phillip, Jr.	Hume, Elizabeth	Sept. 9, 1782
Spring, Nicholas (Spring)	Butcher, Catherine	Aug. 20, 1771
Stanford, James	Burroughs, Judith	Feb. 23, 1790
Stanton, William	Blackwell, Lucy	Sept. 24, 1773
Stark, William	Smith, Ann	Jan. 17, 1793
Stevenson, Benjamin	Ball, Peggy	Feb. 13, 1793
Stark, James	Duncan, Elizabeth	Dec. 18, 1799
Stephenson, Samuel	Hogan, Barbara	August 10, 1786
Stevens, Allen	Jones, Elizabeth	Feb. 21, 1795
Stevens, James	Chadwell, Cinthia	Dec. 23, 1792
Stevson (or Stenson), James	Ball, Judith	Jan. 14, 1800
Stevenson, William	Hickman, Sarah	Dec. 24, 1787
Stevenson, William	Cahoon, Prudence	Oct. 15, 1792
Stewart, William (Stewart)	Grigsby, Susannah	March 25, 1770
Stewart, Allen	Grinnan, Sarah	May 28, 1785
Stigler, Price	McCanahan, Jane	April 3, 1796
Stone, Nimrod,	Russell, Sarah	Dec. 18, 1786
Stout, Isaac	Reed, Winny	Jan. 23, 1800
Stribling, Thomas	Ayers, Elizabeth	---No date---
Striker, Henry	Michael, Caty	

Stringfellow, Harry	Brannin, Mary	Jan. 30, 1793
Stringfellow, George	Jennings, Milly	Jan. 18, 1795
Stukle, George	Michael, Jenny	Nov. 21, 1789
Suddith, Levi	Bowers, Margaret	Nov. 25, 1792
Suddith, John	Williams, Nancy	Dec. 25, 1798
Sullivan, Sylvester	McCabe, Hanson	June 3, 1796
Sullivan, William	Jones, Ann	Feb. 20, 1790
Sthard (Southard), Benjamin	Payne, Ann	Dec. 30, 1785
Sutton, John	Lawler, Polly	August 1, 1798
Taylor, Benjamin	Weaver, Catherine	Nov. 30, 1789
Taylor, James	Triplett, Helen	April 2, 1794
Taylor, Jesse	Embry, Sarah	Dec. 5, 1795
Taylor, John	Buckner, Catherine Taliaferrio	Nov. 22, '
Taylor, John	Doleas, Polly	Oct. 24, 1796
Taylor, Thomas	Gore, Caty	Nov. 26, 1794
Thayer, William	Jones, Hannah	Jan. 16, 1789
Thomas, Benjamin	Glascock, Catherine	Feb. 14, 1788
Thomas, Daniel	Moss, Mary	Dec. 22, 1795
Thomas, Elisha	Glascock, Alice	May 24, 1788
Thomas, James	Stevenson, Peggy	Feb. 29, 1788
Thomas, William	Weeden, Polly	May 9, 1791
Thompson, Aaron	Elliott, Sary	Dec. 7, 1791
Thornton, Thomas	Hampton, Elizabeth	Dec. 16, 1795
Threlkyold, William	Spiller, Chloe	Feb. 5, 1787
Tinsal, John	Button, Sarah	Dec. 10, 1785
Tolles, Micajah	Babson, Polly	Dec. 21, 1796
Tolles, Reuben	Tarlton, Sarah	May 15, 1796
Tolls, John	Dobell, Elizabeth	Nov. 7, 1799

Tollos, Reuben	Tarlton, Sarah	March 13, 1798
Tollos, Jonathan	Henderson, Elizabeth	July 23, 1798
Tollos, William	Bonam (Bonum), Diana	Oct. 19, 1790
Tollos, Stephen	Crosby, Ann	Nov. (?) 5, 1788
Tomlin, William	Rogers, Kissy	March 23, 1789
Tolton, James	West, Jane	May 4, 1796
Tracy, William	Grigsby, Finny	April 29, 1789
Tracy, Philip	Frie, Susan	Jan. 23, 1800
Triplott, John	Morehead, Susan	May 9, 1791
Triplott, Reuben	French, Margaret	July 8, 1790
Tippett (or Triplott), William	Hill, Sarah	Jan. 14, 1765
Triplott, William	Morehead, Eliz.	Dec. 12, 1785
Triplott, Lawerence	Triplott, Benedicto	April 24, 1786
Triplott, William	Rector, Darius (Lucas)	Jan. 9, 1800
Trueman, John	Embrey, Leanna	Jan. 2, 1796
Turley, John	Squire, Susannah	March 18, 1783
Turner, Alexander	Rollins, Peggy	May 17, 1786
Turner, James	Bobell, Ann	Dec. 6, 1792
Turner, John	James, Franky	Dec. 31, 1798
Turner, John	Bailey, Jenny	June 12, 1782
Turner, Thomas	Randolph, Elizabeth	Sept. 1, 1798
Tullos, Rodham	Finnie, Ann	Aug. 21, 1764
Tyler, Benjamin	Foote, Mary	April 9, 1764
Underwood, Anthony	Douglas, Sarah	Dec. 11, 1798
Underwood, John	Teagle, Susan	April 3, 1789
Utterback, Benjamin	Snelling, Elizabeth	Nov. 15, 1780
Utterback, Charles	Nelson, Jemina	Sept. 7, 1789

Vowls, John	Battaly, Hannah	Feb. 26, 1781
Vorris, Thaddeus	Brown, Elizabeth	Dec. 5, 1794
Waddell, William	White, Ann	Oct. 31, 1786
Waddell, Mathew	Waddell, Elizabeth	May 21, 1789
Wake, John	Grigsby, Mary	August 24, 1766
Walpole, Edward	Chinn, Ann	June 19, 1772
Wallor, Charles	Crosby, Mary	March 9, 1772
Waugh, Tyler	Crump, Mary	August 23, 1773
Wardon, Elisha	Dearing, Fanny	March 27, 1798
Wardon, Henry	Ford, Ann	Jan. 12, 1790
Warden, John	Elliott, Ann	Jan. -- 1795
Waters, Thomas	Ashby, Ann	Oct. 18, 1796
Welch, Thomas	Turty, Nancy	March 29, 1797
Welch, William	Congrove, Lydia	Sept. 29, 1788
Welch, Sylvester	Glascock, Am.	March 14, 1798
Welch, William	Moore, Margaret	Feb. 3, 1795
Welch, John	White, Elizabeth	Dec. 26, 1796
Watts, Francis	Foley, Sarah	Oct. 16, 1777
Weaver, Jacob	Newman, Molly	-- 8, 1792
Webb, Isaac	Riley, Betsy	March 28, 1793
Weedon, Nathaniel	Smith, Mary	Sept. 18, 1782
West, Charles	Withers, Sally	June 20, 1785
West, Benjamin	Wrenn, Elizabeth	Sept. 10, 1786
Wey, Amos	Fletcher, Lydia	July 27, 1795
Wey, Henry	Crupper, Molly	Feb. 15, 1790
Wey, John	Atterburn, Polly	Oct. 20, 1795
Whalen, Patrick	Leach, Susannah	July 28, 1775
Wharton, Samuel	Bowman, Rebecca	Dec. 1, 1783

Wheatley, George	Darnall, Diana	Feb. 10, 1760
White, John	Dairs, Mary	Feb. 19, 1798
White, William	McDonald, Lydia	Jan. 1, 1798
White, Thomas	Finch, Elisabeth	Oct. 16, 1798
White, Goring	Duncan, Leanna	Jan. 19, 1789
White, John	Bailey, Ann	Jan. 7, 1783
Whitecotton, Harris	Shumate, Margaret	May 4, 1790
Whitacre, Caleph	Whitacre, Kosiah	May 1, 1793
Wicks, Thomas	Jacobs, Moring	Feb. 6, 1795
Wickliffe, Robert	Hardin, Mary	June 18, 1759
Wickliffe, David	Seaton, Margaret	Oct. 28, 1782
Wigginton, Benjamin	Thornberry, Mary	Oct. 1, 1783
Wilkinson, John	Moffett, Lucretia	Dec. 21, 1782
Williangham, William	Corder, Eve	Oct. 10, 1793
Wells (or Wills), John	Smith Susannah	Feb. 19, 1787
Wilkins, Thomas	Weeks, Peggy	Feb. 20, 1800
Wilkinson, Joshua	Thompson, Ann	Oct. 3, 1798
Willoughby, Elijah	Leachman, Susannah	Oct. 18, 1787
Willoughby, John	Leachman, Mary	Oct. 28, 1787
Willoughby, David	Griffin, Margaret	Nov. 2, 1797
Williams, John Pope	Minter, Hannah	June 19, 1773
Williams, William	Settle, Elizabeth	Dec. 31, 1767
Williams, Richard	Hudnall, Molly	Dec. 27, 1790
Williams, George	Sharp, Ann	Oct. 28, 1782
Williams, Paul	Wheatley, Sarah	June 22, 1786
Wilson, Alexander	Olivor, Mary	Dec. 8, 1786
Winn, Minor	Withors, Betty	Oct. 17, 1766

Winn, James	Withers, Hannah	March 3, 1767
Withers, William	Rosser, Hannah	March 18, 1769
Withers, Jesse	Porter, Catherine	August 6, 1789
Withers, James	Pickett, Sarah	Nov. 19, 1773
Withers, James	Jennings, Cloe	Nov. 4, 1775
Withers, William	Barber, Elizabeth	March 17, 1777
Withers, John	Wood, Elizabeth	Dec. 23, 1795
Withers, John	Rose, Susannah	Sept. 6, 1796
Withers, James	Mauzy, Betsy	Sept. 6, 1798
Withers, William	Ashby, Patty	March 28, 1786
Withers, Enoch	Chinn, Jenny	May 18, 1786
Withers, Benjamin	Robinson, Nancy	Feb. 24, 1783
Wood, Thomas	Buckman, Sarah	Aug. 27, 1759
Wood, John	Maddux, Margaret	April 26, 1792
Wood, James	Evans, Elizabeth	Sept. 3, 1786
Wood, Dickinson	Withers, Hannah	Dec. 24, 1793
Wolfe, Jacob	Mason, Mary	Jan. 4, 1798
Wood, Mark	Bashaw (?), Mary	July 12, 1787
Wrenn, Jeremiah	McDonald, Eleanor	Feb. 7, 1798
Wrenn, Daniel	Bishop, Elizabeth	Feby. 11, 1796
Wrenn, Thomas	Turley, Nancy	March 14, 179
Wright, James	Duncan, Mary	Dec. 8, 1763
Wright, David	Martin, Nancy	Jan. 28, 1790
Wright, John	Mason, Ann	Nov. 5, 1790
Wright, Elijah	Brannin, Polly	Jan. 17, 1794
Wharton, Long	Dillard, Molly	Sept. 22, 1792
Willingham, John	Borden, Sarah	Dec. 23, 1792

Young, James	Peters, Sally	Sept. 22, 1795
Young, John	Singleton, Elizabeth	Feb. 9, 1788
Young, Nimrod	Settle, Elizabeth	Feb. 25, 1789
Youngblood, William	Carter, Elinor	-------1786

Omitted Marriage Bonds

Rossey, Thomas	Fishback, Lydia	Dec. 24, 1796
Taylor, Raleigh	Waddell, Elizabeth	Sept. 10, 1792
Taylor, William	Drummond, Susannah	Sept. 5, 1778

PENSION RECORDS

NAME	RANK	SERVICE	WHEN PLACED ON PENSION ROLL	COMMENCE- MENT OF PENSION	
Beale, Richard E,	Pri.	Va. Mil.	12.17.1832	3.4.1831	74
Blackwell, David	Pri.	Va. Mil	4.24.1833	3.4.1831	84
Canady, John	Seaman	Va. St. Navy	2.15.1833	3.4.1831	70
Combs, Robert	Pr.	Va. Conti.	6.17.1833	7.4.1833	81
Edmonds, David	Pri.	Va. St. Troop	11.21.1833	3.4.1831	77
Ethell, Anthony	Pri.	Va. Conti.	6.8.1833	3.4.1833	77
Groves, Philip	Pri.	Va. Mil.	10.11.1833	3.4.1831	78
Jeffries, Alexander	Pri.	Va. St. Troops	2.5.1833	3.4.1831	72
Kemper, Charles	Pri.	Va. Mil.	2.26.1833	3.4.1831	78
Merry, Philip	Pri.	Va. Mil	4.4.1834	3.4.1831	85
Moffitt, Jesse	Pri.	Va. St. Troop	4.18.1833	3.4.1831	75
Monroe, George	Pri.	Va. St. Troops	5.23.1833	3.4.1831	71
MCClanahan, William	Pri.	Va. Conti.	4.1.1833	3.4.1831	72
Morrison, Edward	Pri.	Va. Cav.	7.19.1833	3.4.1831	76
Murphy, John	Pri.	Va. St. Troops	4.18.1833	3.4.1831	102
Payne, William	Sergt.	Va. Mil.	2.28, 1831	3.4.1831	75
Payne, Augustine	Pri.	Va. Mil.	2.25.1833	3.4.1831	72
Payne, William Capt.	Capt.	Va. St. Troop	2.23.1833	3.4.1831	80
Obannon, Thomas	Pri.	Va. Mil.	8.18.1833	3.4.1831	76
Rowles, William	Pri,	Va. St. Troops	3.20.1833	3.4.1831	75
Rawles, Kenag	Pri.	Va. Mil.	10.4.1833	3.4.1831	70
Riddle, William	Pri.	Va. Mil	10.12.1833	3.4.1831	84
Thompson, John	Pri.	S. Car. Mil.	1.24.1833	3.4.1831	77

NAME	RANK	SERVICE	WHEN PLACED ON ROLL	COMMENCEMENT OF PENSION	AGE
Tomlin, William, Sr.	Capt.	8.21.1832 Va. Conti.		3.4.1831	76
Welch, Sylvester	Pri.	Va. Conti.	4.2.1833	3.4.1831	79
Withers, Spencer	Sergt.	Va. Conti.	4.10.1833	3.4.1831	88
Withers, Jesse	Pri.&Sergt	Va. Hil.	9.26.1833	3.4.1831	74
Wickliffe, David	Pri.	Va. Conti.	3.11.1833	3.4.1831	80

CEMETERY INSCRIPTIONS
Warrenton
Fauquier County
Virginia.

Adams, Virginia, daughter of Dr. John and Mary Adams. 1842-1897 (Buried on Sower lot.)

Adams, Sarah, wife of John T. Adams, died 1850.

Andrew, Alice, daughter of M.B. Goyston. 1813-1874.

Allen, Edmund, 1810-1884.

Allen, Margaret E., wife of Edmund Allen. 1814-1883.

Armitage, Mary Ann, wife of Robert Mandeville Hamilton, born Accomac Co., Virginia. 1797-1891.

Baylor, Fanny Courtneay. 1824-1842.

Baylor, Anne Bridges, relict of John Walker Baylor, born in Clark Co., Virginia, daughter of George Fitzhugh, of Fauquier County, Virginia. 1784-1866.

Bartenstein, Elizabeth, died 1878, aged 56 years.

Bartenstein, Ferdinane, born in Germany. 1816-1864.

Bartenstein, Sarah Fitzhugh, Oct. 1849 - 1921.

Bartenstein, Edward. 1858-1913.

Bartenstein, Miss L.A., died 1887, aged 23 years.

Barry, Robert. 1839-1912

Barry, Julia. 1843-1910

Barker (Barler), Edward, born in England, 1865, died 1921.

Barker, Lillie Maddux. 1863-1928

Bartlett, John. 1813-1882

Bartlett, Mary Ann. 1919-1876

Bartlett, Martha Ann, 1842-1879

Becksler, William. 1841-1910

Bendall, Virginia Stone, wife of R.T. 1840-1927

Bendall, Virginius Oldner, son of R.T. and Virginia. 1863-1900

Bentles, Annie E., died 1818, aged 25 years.

Peckham, John G. and wife Mary, children, Mary and Alexander- no dates.

Blackwell, John Davenport, A.M. D.D. 1822-1887

Blackwell, Frances Grayson Smith, wife of John Davenport Blackwell. 1848-1924

Blackwell, Eleanor Foote, dau. of John D. and Frances. 1875-1912

Blackburn, John. 1840-1927

Boorman, Elizabeth Duvall, wife of Robert, died 1921.

Brown, F. Turner. 1829-1907

Brown, Hannah. 1823-

Brown, W. Judson. 1834-1902

Brown, Anabelle. 1846-1924

Brown, Lillie Maddux. 1920-1923

Brown, William. 1866-1929

Brown, Florence H., wife of William. 1869-1912

Browning, Maria, wife of Henry H. 1846-1904

Browning, Henry R. 1837-1900

Brooke, Francis Calvin. 1858-1911

Brooke, Annie Amelia, dau. of James V. and Mary E. Brooke, died 1876, aged 18 years.

Brooke, Richard Harris (?). 1847-1920

Brooke, James V. 1824-1888

Brooke, Virginia, dau. of Reuben and Ann S.H. Brooke, died 1884. (See Payne)

Brooke, Virginia Dandridge, dau. of H.L. and Virginia Brooke. Died Sept. 1846

Butts, J-Anna (or Joanna), dau. of Francis and Emma Butts, consort of Rev. J.D. Blackwell. 1834-1868.

Butler, Addie Ingle .   1831-1906

Butler, George Griffin. 1822-1908

Butler, Alice.   --- Feb.23, 1922

Butler, Helen V. Died 1925

Bullock, Capt. W.E. born in Northumberland, England, March 30, 1845 -1916.

Bullock, Lilly, wife of Capt. W.E., born in England, died in Shelton, Washington, 1935.

Bywater, Mamie. 1833-1923

Bywater, Mildred. 1908-1927

Carter, Cassius. 1835-1914

Carter, Fanny Foote Green, wife of Cassius Carter. 1839-1893

Carter, Francis Scott, died 1921, aged 53 years.

Carter, Shirley, M.D. 1835-1928

Carter, Richard. 1826-1882

Carter, Isaiah. 182- - 1874

Carter, Henry L. 1814-1905.

Carr, Herbert Henry, 5th son of William Carr, born at Black Heath, England, March 7, 1867, died 1899, Fauquier County, Va.

Chilton, Joseph. Died 1841, aged 70 years.

Chilton, Lucy Stephen. 1810-1904

Ann Chilton Johnson -- See Johnson.

Cockrill, R.A. 1852-1916

Cockrill, Mary E. 1851-1917

Cockrill, Hugh S. 1883-1883

Connelly, Cornelius, born Cork, Ireland, died 1899, aged 65 years.

Crown, Rev. James Henry, born 1834, in Montgomery Co. Maryland, died 1890.

   Crown, Hannah, wife of Rev. James Crown. 1845-1927

Day, Alexander. 1843-1862

Day, Douglas. 1829-1875

Day, Virginia Turner, wife of Douglas Day. 1839-1910

Day, Baldwin. 1797-1852

Day -- (See Swift)

Dads, Baylor Gurynnetta, dau. of J.W.Tyler. Died 1883. See Tyler.

Dent, William. 1807-1890

Dent, Mary Ann. 1811-1891

De Shields, James. 1804-1862

De Shields, Elizabeth. 1811-1884

Drysdale, Christian, died June, 1901

Drysdale, Thomas. 1876-1880

Douglas, Martin Guthrie, born in Maryland. 1869-1920

Edwards, W.W. 1812-1900

Edwards, Ann, died 1902, aged 82 years.

Edmonds, Edward G. 1836-1897

Edmonds, Adeline, wife of Edward G. 1834-1907

English, Maria C. daughter of James and Elizabeth Roe English. 1826-1903

English, Elizabeth Roe. 1790-1881

English, Joseph Marion, son of James and Elizabeth R. English. 1824-1861

Evans, Frances. 1836-1906

Evans, Sarah, 1797-1887

Evans, Mildred Moore Campbell. 1850-1866 (See Campbell)

Fallen, Patrick. Died 188-- aged 84 years.

Fallen, Margaret, died 1887---

Finks, John W. 1818-1877

Finks, Lucy A. 1822-1911

Finks, Ann Rebecca, adopted daugter of John W. and Lucy Finks. 18--- 1853

Fisher, Fannie. 1849-1815

Fisher, Elizabeth. 1810-1895

Fisher, John. 1801-1884

Fisher, Marh H. 1839-1907

Fisher, Robert W. 1835-1908

Fisher, Robert. 1888-1923
A large stone with name of FISHER upon it and the graves of Annie E. Johnson (1845-1899) and J.D.Ashton (1842-1914)

Fletcher, Mrs. Louisa. Died 1893, aged 75 years.

Fletcher, A.D. 1814-1890

Fletcher, Manley. 1845-1870

Fletcher, V.A. "In Memory of Aunt Nish." Died 1849, aged 45 years.

Fletcher, Manley. Died 1873, aged 7 months.

Fletcher, Hugh. 1877-1905

Fletcher, Thaddeus Norris. 1843-1920

Fletcher, Georgie O'Latham, wife of Thaddeus N. 1847-1895
(On Fletcher lot is grave of Sallie W. Withers, wife of Albert. 1850-1878

Flynn, Rachol Hunter. 1845-1919

Flynn, Mable. 1884-1916

Flynn --- 1838-1910

Fontaine, Elizabeth. 1845-1864

Fowler, Col. W.F. 1810-1896

Francis, Fannie. 1830-1901

Furlong, Isabella. 1857-1915

Furlong, Edward P. 1834-1854

Gallaway, C.F. 1842----

Gallaway, Susannah. 1841-1901

hlette, Mrs. Phebe. Died 1889, aged 62 years.

Glascock, Helen Smith. 1872-1917

Glascock, Louisa, wife of John Samuel Glascock, and dau. of Ludwell and Agnes Lake. 1830-1892

Glascock, John Samuel, 1828-1886, son of Henry and Jane Glascock.

Goodwin, Dr. Le Baron. April 21, 1800 - Nov. 7, 1859
On Goodwin lot stones broken and only word ANN legible.

Gowhig, William. April, 1833 - July, 1919.

Gowhig, Hannah. Jan. 1840-July, 1916

Gowhig, Mary H. Dau. of William and Hannah. Oct. 2, 1863 -1913

Gowhig, William H. 1873-1890

Gowhig, Bridget. 1815-1831

Gowhig, Patrick John. 1857-1898

Gowhig, Dennis. 1813-1890

Gowhig, Ellen, dau. of Dennis and Bridget, born at Melrose Station, 1855-1879

Gowhig, William, son of Dennis and Bridget, July 1864-1884

Graham, Jmaes M. Dec. 1844-1916

Graham, J. Barbour, wife of James M. Died 1904, aged 57 years.

Gray, Mary E. 1848-1912

Gray, Emma E. 1886-1915

Gray, Mrs. Virginia. Died 1904, aged 44 years.

Gray, Newton Lee. 1889-1919

Gray, James William. May 16, 1854-1927

Gaskin, Sophrona. 1850-1931 (See Triplett)

Green, Bernard. 1842-1902

Green, Thomas. 1838-1899

Green, Charles T. 1820-1897

Green, Lucy, wife of Charles T. 1831-1875

Guthrie, Eliza D. Died 1855, aged 77 years.

Hamilton, Hugh. 1841 - 1928

Hamilton, Isabella Voss. 1840-1927

Hamilton, Totty Peace. 1874-1905

Hamilton, Marianna Scott. Died 1918, in 90th year of age.

Hamilton, George Stanton. 1830-1912

Harris, James K. Died 1862, aged 18 years. 5th Texas Regiment, mortally wounded at 2nd Battle of Mannassa.

Harris, H. Ashby. 1862-1928

Hays, Edward. 1865-1878

Helm, Fraspins. Born in Kentucky. Died 1872.

Helm, Mary, wife of Fraspins. 1813-1882

Helm, Eramus. 1819-1864

Helm, Virginia, wife of Eramus. 1812-1852

Helm, Virginia Asquith. Died 1841, aged 18 years.

Helm, Edward. 1841-1863

Helm, Robert. 1845-1864

Helm, Frances. 1848 - 1972

Heflin, Alfred, son of Lawson and A. E. 1889-1908

Heflin, Ann Eliza. 1804 (?) -1895

Hendricks, Elizabeth (Sue Pollock). 1843-1914

Hicks, Robert. 1831-1920. Major of C.S.A.

Hicks, Nannie Fitzhugh Randolph, wife of Maj. Robert I. Hicks. 1838-1893

Holt, Fred. Died 1910

Holtzclaw, Elizabeth. 1820-

Holtzclaw, George. 1815-1885

Holtzclaw, 1868-1878

Holtzclaw, Howard. 1868-1878

Holtzclaw, Frank. 1854-1865

Holtzclaw, Amon (Almon) Seabury. 1867-1889

Holtzclaw, Willie Baldwin. 1851-1912

Holtzclaw, Grace. 1857-----

Hornor, Elizaboth. 1811 - 1850

Hornor, Joseph. 1807-1886

Hornor, William .-----

Hornor, Mary McClenachan Robb, wife of William. 1828-1916

Hornor, Seignora Peyton, died 1876.

Hornor, Dr. Frederick. Assistant surgeon, U.S.N. 1828-1902

Horner, Maria Sherman, wife of Dr. Fred. Horner. Oct. 5, 1849-1920

Horner, Richard Henry. 1839-1899 (C.S.A.)

Horner, Virginia Cary, wife of Richard Henry Horner. 1844-1904

Horner, Frances Scott, wife of Robert Downman. 1837-1900

Horner, Ann Maria Lovell, wife of Dr. Frederick Horner. 1816-1898

Horner, Frederick. 1816-188-

Horner, Gustavus Richard, son of William and Mary Edmonds Horner. 1804-1892

Horner, Mary Agnes, wife of Gustavus R. and dau. of Charles and Emeline Byrnes. 1815-1884

Horner, Charles Gustavus, son of Gustavus and Mary A. Byrnes Horner. 1869-1914

Horner, Alfred Byrnes, son of Gustavus and Mary A. Pyrnes Horner. 1861-1934

Horner, Anne Brown. 1836-1921

Howey, John A. Died 1900, aged 87 years.

Horner, Robert Braxton. 1867-1910

Horner, Robert Littleton. 1825-1910

Horner, Ellen Ashton. Died 1876.

Hurst, Rosalie, wife of George. Died 1897

Hutton, Margaret. 1827-1908

Hyde, Ellen. Died 1902, aged 65 years.

Hyde, Ellen, wife of Philip. (Same as above)

Hyde, Philip. Born in County Cork, Ireland. 1829-1893

Hyde, Mannie (sister), died in 22nd year of age.

Isabell, Jonas, born in the North of England. Died 1850, aged 88 years.

James, John. 1819-1892. (On Smith lot)

Jameson, Frederick G. 1915-1919

Jeffries, James Payne. Died 1908, aged 55 year.

Jeffries, Mary H. Wyer, wife of James P., dau. of Henry and Anne Powell Wyer. 1856-1920. (See Wyer)

Jeffries, James Payne, son of James P. and M.H.Jeffries. 188-1890

Jeffries, James Penfield, son of James P. and M.H. Jeffries. 1892-1925

Jennings, Mrs. Lucy, relict of Thomas O. Jones, Esq. Died Jan. 25, 1862, aged 70 years.

Jennings, Louisa A. wife of W.A.Jennings, dau. of Dr. Turner and Harriett Adams of Zanesville, Ohio. 1840-1904

Jennings, Dr. Louis. Died 1860, aged 32 years.

Jolly, Annie Owen, wife of J.D.Jolly. 1867-1917

Jones, Richard B. 1852 -1915

Jones, Honora, wife of Richard B. 1853-1931

Jones, Elizabeth. Born July 20, 1856; Died Oct. 27, 1914

Jones, John J. 1856-1906

Jones, Infant of John and Elizabeth. 1885

Johns, Edward Lovell, son of Edward L. and Sarah, 1864-1906

Johnson, Cora, wife of T.S. Johnson. 1845-1904

Johnson, Mrs. James. Died 1838, aged 30 years.

Johnson, Ida M. wife of T.F. 1869-1920

Johnson, Eppa H., son of B.M. and L.F. 1871-1903(?)

Johnson, Harry Mauzy. 1845-1908

Johnson, Katherine, dau. of P.L. 1878-1899

Johnson, Iram (?). 1875-1876

Johnson, James F. B.&D. 1887

Keith, Isham, son of Thomas and grandson of Rev. James Keith, of Scotland. 1801-1862

Keith, Juliet Chilton, wife of Isham Keith, and dau. of Joseph Chilton. 1800-1887

Keith, Sarah, wife of Isham Keith. 1837-1912

Keith, James S. , son of Isham Keith and wife Sarah A. Keith. 1869-1918 (See Chilton)

Kemper - "Memory of Father and Mother."

Kemper, Col. John Kemper. 1768-1856

Kemper, Martha. 1769-1847

King, William . 1825-1907

King, Josie E., wife of F.A.Merriman (See Merriman)

King, Edwin B., Jr., only son of Edwin B. and Mary S.F.King. 1911-1915

Kirby, John G. 1876-1933

Kirby, Caroline Sims, wife of John G. 1870-1934

Kirby, Virginia Sims. 1898-1924 (See Sims)

Kirby, Capt. James. 1838-1906

Kirby, Julia C. (Claggett). 1844-1921

Kirkpatrick, Enoch J. 1846-----

Kirkpatrick, Delia Catherine, wife of Enoch, 1841-1911

Lee, Charles. Died 1815, aged 57 years. U.S.Stty. Gen. 1797-1801 (See Pollock)

Lee, Julian. 1840- 1901

Lee, Meta Wallace. 1850-188?

Lake, Isaac. 1837-1905

Lake, John. 1840-1913. Capt. C.S.A.

Legg, Daisy. Died 1908, aged 24 years.

Limerick, Mary, wife of James -- 1837-- illegible.

Lomax, Lindsay Lunsford. 1835-1913. Major Gen. of Army of Northern Virginia. 1835-1913

Lomax, Elizabeth Winter Payne, wife of above. 1850-1932

Luke, Elizabeth. Died 22 February, 1908.

Lunceford, Benjamin. 1837-1900

Lunceford, Amanda. 1841-1898

Lunceford, B.F. 1856-1891

Maddux, Thomas L., son of James H. and Jane Maddux. 1856-1885

Maddux, Theodore, son of James and Jane. 1859-1887

Maddux, Jmaes Henry. March 14, 1818 -1899

Maddux, James Kerfoot. 1853-1930. Cora Virginia Johnson on Maddux lot.

Marr, Margaret, 1830-1903

Marr, Sally, eldest dau. of John and C. Marr. 1817-1895

Marr, John. June 6, 1788-1848

Marr, Catherine Inman, wife of John Marr. 1797-1878

Marr, Wallace Marion. Died Nov. 26, 1844, aged 24 years.

Marr, John. 1825-1861

Marr, James Ripon. 1832-1879

Marr, Frances Harrison. 1835-1918

Marr, Jane Blackburn. Feb.4, 1840-1929. "The last of her generation and a noble representative of Old Virginia."

Marr, Margaret Moore. 1830-1903

Marr, John Quincy. 1825-1861. C.S.A.

Marr, John Blackburn. 1840-1927

Marshall, R.I. Taylor. 1835-1862

Marshall, Maria Rose, wife of Alexander Marshall. 1803-1904

Marshall, Alexander J. 1803-1862

Mann, Sally A. 1832-1903

Mann, Joel. 1822-1912

Mann, Jesse L., son of Joel. Died 1888, aged 22 years.

McLearen, Thomas Coleman. 1812-1886

Maxheimer, Joseph. 1849-1916

Maxheimer, Elizabeth. B., wife of Joseph. Born in Scotland. 1851-1912

Mayhugh, John Thomas. 1864-1928

Merriam, Fred K.- 1833-1833

Merriam, Josie E. King, wife of F.A.

Merriam, Josephine. 1855-1888 (See King)

Mountjoy, S.F. 1847-1922

Mountjoy, M.S. 1826-1911

Mountjoy, J.W. 1838-1922

Mountjoy, R.R. Born March 15, 1842. Died 1864. Capt. of Company D, Battalion Virginia Cavalry, Mosby men. Monument erected by his comrades. C.S.A.

Muller, William, born in England. 1810-1884

Muller, Susan, born in London, England. 1836-1895

Muller, Ernest, aged 5 years.

Muller, Frank. 1862-1917

Muller, William. Born in Devonshire, England, Jan.2, 1866; died in New York, 1892.

Nagle, Mrs. Mary. April 20, 1821-1896

Neal, Ann Amelia, wife of George Neal. 1835-1886

Neal, George H. 1829-1891

Nelson, Marvin, 1886-1908

Nelson, Joseph. 1873-1983

Nelson, Nadine. 1879-1883

Nelson, Margurite. 188-1895

Nelson, George W., Jr. 1875-1928

Nelson, Rev. G.W. 1840-1903

Nelson, Mary Scollay, wife of Rev. George W. 1850-1923

Newby, Robert C. 1822-1884

Newby, Georginana, wife of Robert. 1824-1868
(Graves of several children on this lot)

O'HARA, Isabelle Byrne. 1844-1895

O'Hara, Mary Emoline. 1863-1902

O'Reilley, Thomas. 1873-1904

O'Reilley. 1879-1900 (Robert)

O'Reilley, Nicholas. 1876-1894

O'Reilley, Philip. 1866-1887

O'Reilley, Brian. 1868-1886

O'Reilley, Miles. 1886-1 year

O'Reilley, Robert. 1832-1905

O'Reilley, Margaret. 1844-

Page, Sarah E., wife of John. Died 1871, aged 58 years.

Page, John --- illegible.

Page, Helen Stuart. 1839-1858

Palmer, Maj. F. Gendron. Mortally wounded at the 2nd Battle of Manassa. Died Nov. 4, 1862

Parkinson, J.W. 1817-1904

Parkinson. L.A. 1829-1892

Pattie, William. Born 1849; died 1859

Pattie, Otho H.W. 1844-1877

Pattie, C.C. 1654-1878

Pattie, V.A. 1831-1857

Pattie, Jenny, wife of William Pattie. 1822-1859

Payne, William Winter. 1807-1874

Payne, John D. H.D. Born in Tuscumbia, Alabama, died in Fauquier County, Virginia, 1881.

Payne, Rev. T.Alexander, son of Inman and Mary Payne. 1863-1898

Payne, Inman H. 1822-1905

Payne, Mary Ann, wife of Inman Payne. 1824-1900

Payne, John Massie, son of Inman. 1852-1921

Payne, Markham Brooks, son of Inman Payne. 1865-1902

Payne, Alexander Dixon, son of Richard and Alice Fitzhugh Dixon Payne. 1837-1893

Payne, William Fitzhugh. "Not for empire or renown, but for right and commonwealth." Son of Arthur Morson and Mary Mason Fitzhugh, born Jan. 27, 1830; died March, 1904. He entered the Confederate Army as Capt. of Black Horse Troop, and rose to be Brig. Gen. of the 2nd Brigade of Fitzhugh Lee's division.

Payne, Mary B., wife of Gen. W.H.F. Payne, dau. of Col. William Winter and Minerva Winston Payne. 1831-1920

Payne, Charles Edward Fitzhugh. 1841-

Payne, Jeans Morrison Brook, wife of G.B.F. 1850-1921

Payne, Charles Fitzhugh. 1877-1928. 1st Lt. Aero Squadron, A.E.F.

Payne, Sarah Robb Tyler, dau. of A.H. (?) and Mary E. 1865-1875

Payne, Harry Fitzhugh, son of Brig. Gen. W,H,F, Payne and Mary Winston Payne. 1857-1933

Payne, John Winston, son of William H. and Mary, b. 1858-1937

Payne, John Daniel. 1862-1901

Payne, Minerva Winston, wife of William Winter Payne, dau. of Col. John Winston, of Alabama. 1811-1882

Pierson, Lizzie, wife of Rev. William Pierson, of New York. Died 1880, aged 24 years.

Pollock, Rev. A.D.   1807-1890

Pollock, Elizabeth Gordon, 1812-1894(?), wife of Rev. A.D. Pollock, daughter of Charles Lee. (See Lee)

Pollock, Elizabeth Hendrick, daughter of Rev. A.D. Pollock.   1843-1914

Pollock, Charles Lee. Died 1888, aged 39 years.

Pollock, Thomas Gordon. Died 1863, aged 24 years - killed at Gettysburg.

Portman, Frederick Arthur Berkeley.   1867-1907

Reed, Margaret.   1810-1385

Richardson, Alexander.   1788-1862

Riley, Annie. Died 1888, aged 75 years.

Robinson, Sarah E. Died 1903, aged 63 years.

Robinson, William E.   1842-1915.   C.S.A.

Russell, Samuel and Eliza --- inscriptions illegible.

Rush, Peyton L. (father).   1835-1896

Rush, Lucy E. (mother).   1834-1911

Rush, Charles C.   1858-1931

Rush, Mary E.   1858-1931

Saunders, John A. Company "D", Mosby Virginia Cavalry, C.S.A.

Saunders, Thomas .   "   "   "   "

Saunders, T.E. 1822 -1906

Saunders, Mary E. , wife of Thomas. 1820-1887

Scott, John Gordon, son of Col. John Scott and wife Augusta Caskie. 1859-1932

Scott, John, son of Judge John Scott and wife Elizabeth Pickett. 1820-1907

Scott, Lucinda. Died 1850

Sedwick, Cora Elizabeth. Jan. 17, 1857 -1869

Sedwick, Benjamin. Died 1875, aged 64 years.

Schwab, Anton. 1834-1906

Schwab, Susan E. 1837-1930

Schwab, Joseph, son of Anton Schwab. 1863-1886

Shellman, John. Died 1862, aged 20 years.

Shepherd, John. Died 1849

Sims, Marian Louise. 1848-1907

Sims, Alice Mosby. 1865-1928

Smith, John Thomas. Died 1872, aged 56 years.

Smith, Annie E. Jan. 11, 1801-1881

Smith, John. 1797-1863

Smith, George Summer. 1849-1819

Smith, Amanda, wife of P.A.L. 1821-1903

Smith, Frank P. 1854-1907

Smith, William. 1866-1908

Smith, Jenny. 1849-19---

Smith, John. March 3, 1817 (or 1812) - Feb. 11, 1892

Sinclair, Maria Louisa. Sept. 13, 1829-1889

Sinclair, Ann Maria. Died 1892- aged 69 years

St. Clair, Cornelia. 1858-1915

St. Clair, Robert. 1856-1915

Sower, William Summer. 1869-1931

Sower, Mary. 1844-1922

Sower, Richard. Dec. 1837-1910. C.S.A.

Spellman, Annie Hayward, wife of H. Conway Spellman. Died June 22, 1906.

Spellman, H. Conway. Died Feb. 1917

Spellman, Hayward North. June 1889-1935. (World War soldier)

Spicer, Maude. 1875-1913

Spicer, Wade. 1871-1909

Sudduth, Mary. Died 1851, aged 33 years.

Sullivan, Maggie, daughter of Dennis and Ellen Sullivan. 1876-1892

Tongue, T. William. 1846-1918

Tongue, Rosa Neal. Died 1928

Tongue, Johnzie. 1845- 1925

Tongue, Frances. 1818-1891

Tongue, James R. 1809-1881

TONGUE -- "In memory of Johnzie Tongue, Priscilla Tongue, Thomas L. Tongue, Martha Tongue, Ann L. Tongue. 1798-1872.

Triplett, P.H. 1849-1919

Triplett, Landiss (?). 1853-1881

Triplett, Spillman L. 1901-1928

Triplett, Arthur W. 1846-1927

Triplett, Ella, wife of Arthur W. Triplett. 1843-1908

Turner, Harriett, wife of late Dr. John A. Turner, Dec. 27, 1884, aged 77 years.

Tyler, Constance Horton. 1848-1922

Tyler, Guennetta Baylor Dade, daughter of John Webb Tyler. Died 1883

Utterback, William Warren, son of John and Mary. 1890-1920

Utterback, Annie. Died in Lynchburg, 1905.

Utterback, Addison D. Died 1896

Utterback, Virginia. Died 1920

Vose, Laura G., wife of F.G.Vose and sister of F.G.Anderson. Sept. 1865-1918.

Ward, Berkeley. April 1783-1860

Ward, Henry C. 1829-1861. 1st Lt. of Fauquier County Guards. Killed at first Battle of Mannassa.

Ward, Harriett ------ illegible.

Ward, Dr. John. June, 1826-1885

Ward, Mary Grace, widow of Dr. John Ward, born in Baltimore, Maryland; died 1898, in Washington, D.C.

Waller, John Tyler. 1845-1865

Washington, Georgianna Langhorne Baylor, widow of Temple Washington, daughter of Jane Alexander Dade (?) and G -- Walker Baylor. March 13, 1808 - Jan. 14, 1908.

Washington, Estelle ---- inscription illegible.

Wells, H. 1833-1905

White, John L. 1817-1899

White, Gamilla, wife of John White, 1821-1892

White, Charles Mason. 1855-1911

White, Mary, dau. of Charles G. and Helen White, 1888-1890

White, D.B. D. 1893

White, Jane H., wife of D.B. White ---

White, Hamden. 1812-1888

White, Rev. Robert. 1850 -1905

White, Sallie Warren, wife of Rev. Robert White. 1855-1925

Wine, James. 1834-1909

Wine, Sarah G. 1833-1909

Wingfield, Thomas Smith. 1813-1897

Winmill, Albert. 1852-1904

Winmill, Josephine. 1855-1910

Williamson, Louisa R.F. 1852-1933

Williamson, Catherine. Died 1905. This stone was erected in "Loving memory of mother, Susan, and brother, Robert Bruce."

Williamson, Thomas Vowell and Sarah Brook Williamson --------

Williamson, Rev. William. Died 1848, aged 83 years.

Williamson, W.W.   Died 1903

Williamson, Louisa F.   1852-1933

Withers, Sallie W., wife of Albert Withers.   1850-1878

Withers, Dr. Thomas.   1790 (or 1796) -1865

Wise, George C.   1848-1922.   U.S. Navy.

Woodsell, Emma D.   Died 1908, aged 38 years .

Woodsell, Mary.   1878-1918

Woodsell, Martha Clark.   1847-1924

Woodsell, George.   1842-1933

Wood, Daniel.   1852-1924

Wyer, Rev. Henry.   1829-1901

Wyer, Ann E. Powell, wife of Rev. H. Wyer.   1833-1905

Wyer, John Powell, son of Rev. Henry Wyer.   1863-1905

Wyer, Walter Penfield.   1860-1922

Wyer, Henry Halstead, son of Rev. Henry Wyer.   1870-1906

Weaver, Richard.   Died 1862, aged 39 years.   C.S.A.

Washington, Robert.   1812-1852

Washington, Mildred Jane, wife of Robert Washington.   1824-1926.

FAUQUIER COUNTY RENT ROLL

1770

NAMES	ACRES	NAMES	ACRES
Allen, John, dec'd.	1043	Bartell, Thomas	200
Allen, Archibald	188	Bell, Benjamin	160
-- D'Butts	30	Ball, William	600
Allen, Ursley	230	Bailey, John	100
Allen, John	187	Bains, John	183
Allen, William	148	Bell, James	600
Allen, Thomas	187	Bell, John (from Culpepper Co.)	800
Anderson, John	584	Benson, Pane	250
Adams, Isaac	150	Blackmore, Joseph	--
Arnold, John	150	Boswell, George	648
Aris, John	160	Bethell, Thomas	250
Ashby, Capt. John	1055	Bramlett, Reuben	150
Ashby, Nimrod	100	Bramlett, William	123
Ashby (Frederick Co.)	340	Brooks, Humphrey	150
" New deed	424	Bronaugh, Thomas	150
Ashby, John, Jr.	375	Bronaugh, William	410
Ashby, Stephen	135	Bushaw, James	570
Ashby, Robert	916	Buckner, Ruth	1000
Asberry, William	201	Button, Harmon	164
Ayers, Thomas	350	Bullitt, Cuthbert	300
Barber, John	200	Bullitt, Benjamin	300
Barby, Andrew	145	Carr, John	150

Beach, Peter	200
Barker, William	197
Beach, Margaret	135
Brown, John (Heirs)	300
Blackwell, Col. William	538
Blackwell, Joseph	1180
Brooke, William	200
Berryman, Maxmillian	1163
Buttell, Joseph	287
Berry, George	170
Bailey, James	100
Butler, John	423
Bramlett, Henry	250
Bradford, Daniel	810
Basey, Edmond	125
Burdette, Frederick	100
Baisey, John	200
Carom (Carson), Champe	227
Catlett, John	358
Chinn, Thomas	829
Chilton, John	463
Churchill, Henry	200
Churchill, John (chil. of)	1582
Churchill, Armistead	1690
Chapman, Constance	3068
Chichester, Richard (?)	1600
Chichester, William, Charles, John, Stephen & Thos.	765

Conway, Thomas		1648
Conway, William		200
Conyers, John		489
Coppage, William		850
Coppage, Moses		275
Conyers, Samuel		200
Coventon, Richard		150
Cooledge, Judyson		1748
Cortney, William		182
Cortney, John		300
Crockett, James		134
Crosby, George		226
Crump, George		470
Crump, John	188-93	609
Crump, Benjamin		375
Cummins, Simon		150
Darnall, Mathew		223
Darnold (Darnall), Jermi.		600
Darnold, David		150
Delaney, Joseph		680
Dodd, Nathaniel		196
Dodson, George		100
Dodson, William, Sr.		192
Doggett, Bushrod		800
Duncan, John, Sr.		325
Duncan, Joseph		328
Duncan, John		100
Duncan, Charles		242

Duncan, John	188		Gent, George	100
Duncan, John	125		Gent, Widow	639
Duff, James	100		George, Farnis(?)	150
Downman, Raleigh	630		Genn, James Heirs	774
Eustace, William	1960		Gibson, Jonathan	1050
Edmonds, Elias	885		Gibson, William	50
Edmonds, William	500		Glasscock, --	900
Edwards, John	100		Grant, George (Of Fr. George Co.)	100
Embry, Robert	482		Grinnan ----	186
Edwards, Garrett	219		Grigsby, Samuel	177
Eves, Thomas	200		Grant, William	300
Eves, William	100		Green, Duff	570
Etherington, John	200		Gunning, Thomas	150
Ellis, John	---		Grubbs, Richard	207
Ferry, Ann	443		Hall, Widow	200
Fegan, Daniel	130		Harrison, Col. Thomas.	--
Fishback, Phil	257		Harmon, Fishback	179
Fishback, Josiah	257		Harper, John	230
Fishback, Harmon	100		Harrell, Daniel	100
Fishback, John	257		Hackley, Lott	246
Fishback, Frederick	60		Hackley, Richard	100
Flory, Daniel	150		Hackley, Francis	--
Foley, James, Sr.	117 & 300		Hardin, Martin	965
Fox, Samuel	394		Harley, Richard	100
Garner, Charles	100		Henson, Robert	117
Garner, Vinson	400		Helm, Thomas	388
Garner, James	400		Hampton, Ruth	500

Hitt, Peter, Jr.	275	James, Thomas	980
Hitt, Peter, Sr.	200	James, John Capt.	376
Hitt, John, Jr.	83	Jamos, John	50
Hitt, John	216	Jeffries, John	227
Hitt, Joseph	214	Jennings, Augus	308
Hitt, Harmon	500	Jennings, William	31
Hening, George	100	Jett, Francis	150
Hewit, Susannah	200	Johnson, William	100
Hewit, Susannah	150	Johnson, Moses	150
Hogan, William	124	Johnson, Jeffries	1038
Hopper, Blagrove	325	Jones, John	153
Hogan, James	175	Jones, Brenentom (?)	--
Hogan, William	413	Kemper, Peter	298
Hord, Thomas	235	Kemper, Jacob	163
Holtzclaw	185	Kemper, John	363
Holtzclaw, Benjamin	130	Kemper, Harmon	184
Holtzclaw, Henry	987	Kemper, Henry	---
Humston, Edward	175	Kerner, George	180
Hunter, James	200	Kerner, Howson	775
Hudnal, John (Heirs of)	375	Kernes, William	418
Hudnal, Joseph	200	Kirk, William	--
Hudnal, John	125	Lawerence, Edward	317
Hunter, William	400	Lampkins, George	925
Hudnal, Thomas	500	Leach, Joseph	100
Hudnal, William	375	Lewis, Zachariah	268
Jacob, Morris	211	Luttrell, James	124

Luttrell, John	70		Morgan, William	865
Luttrell, Richard	58		Morgan, William	622
Luttrell, Samuel	70		Morgan, James (Heirs)	174
Luttrell, Michael	70		Morgan, John	166
Luttrell, Robert	74		Morehead, Charles	306
Luttrell, Austin	80		Morehead, John (dec'd)	450
Luttrell, Mary	80		Morgan, William, Jr.	147
Luttrell, Susannah	80		Murray, James	630
Marrs, Ann (widow)	1135		McCarty, Jerrett	50
Martin, Henry	163		McClanahan, William	194
Martin, Joseph	150		McCormack, John	100
Martin, Charles	171		McCormack, Stephen	100
Markham, John	100		McKee, John	66
Mathis, Robert (?)	127		Neavil, Capt. George	--
Martin, John	100		Nevill, John (Heirs)	227
Martin, Eve	100		Nevill, Joseph	116
Mathis, Thomas	350		Nelson, John	298
Mausy, Betty	14		Nelson, John, Sr.	-
Mauzy, Henry	434		Nelms (Helms ?), Samuel	112
Mauzy, Henry	220		Newgent (Nugent), Thomas	--
Mauzy, John (Heirs)	590		Newgent, Edward	--
Miller, Simon (dec'd)	575		Newland, Daniel	140
Miller, William	100		Newport, Peter	100
Minter, Joseph	213		Morris, William	--
Morgan, Charles, Sr.	127		Otterback (Utterback), Henry	--
Morgan, Charles, Jr.	500		Otterback, John	80
Morgan, Simon	463		Obannon, William	---

Name	Amount
Obannon, William Mrs.	--- --
Obannon, William, Sr.	----
Obannon, John Jr.	---
Parker, Dr.	452
Page, Thomas	100
Peirce, Peter (Heirs)	70
Peters, John	800
Pickett, William (Exrs.) (Of Culpepper Co.)	500
Porter, Samuel	235
Ransdell, Wharton	896
Randolph, William	680
Ransow (Rousan), John	260
Rector, Nathaniel	100
Rector, Harmon	100
Reiley, Thomas	200
Rector, Henry	100
Rector, Jacob	100
Rector, John	337
Redding, Timothy	60
Robertson, Joseph	100
Routt, John	--
Routt, Peter (of Stafford County)	--
Right (Wright), Capt. John	236
Rousan, William	250
Russell, William	100
Rust, John	200
Savage, Dr. (of Markham)	1834
Scott, Capt. James	2000
Sorows (?) Heirs	----
Sears, John	576
Seirs (Sears), James	122
Settle, George	100
Settle, George	153
Shumate, Daniel	100
Sinckler, John (dec'd.)	213
Settle, William	507
Settle, Joseph	147
Settle, Isaac	22
Singleton, Stanley	200
Smith, Joseph	600
Smith, Thomas	100
Smith, Augustine	255
Smith, James	---
Smith, Joseph	88
Smith, Thomas	100
Smith, William	---
Smith, Alexander (Heirs)	461
Smith, Caleb	75
Smith, John	156
Stephenson, James	268
Snelling, Aquilla	232
Snelling, Benjamin	38
Stewart, James	476
Stone, Thomas	159

Spielman, Jacob (Heirs)	264	William, Jonathan (Heirs)	174
Stone, Thomas	159	Williams, George	134
Stamps, William	630	Williams (One of D. Chambers heirs)	200
Strothers, Daniel	100	Whily (?), Allen	300
Terrall (?), Francis	100	Withers, James	--
Thomas, Jacob	264	Withers, John	500
Thornberry, Thomas	586	Withers, Thomas	718
Thornton, William	55	Withers, William	600
Triplett, William	434	Wilburn, Edward	138
Waugh, William	150	Welthy (?), Widow	134
Waugh, Joseph	600	Wood, Nehemiah	80
Waller, Charles (Heirs)	400	Wood, Joshua	130
Weaver, Elizabeth Ann	160	Wood, Joseph	100
Weaver, John	150	Wright, Capt. John	236
Weaver, Tillman	311	Wright, William	185
Williams, Paul	241	Young, James	250
		Young, Original	159

TENANTS OF THE MANOR OF LEEDS

FAUQUIER COUNTY

1777

Allen, Archibald	100	Ellis, Sarah	105
Allen, John	104	Flinn, Valentine	200
Allen, Reuben	200	Fletcher, William	200
Allen, William	120	Flelkins, William	150
Barbey, Joseph	200	Garrett, A.	200
Barbey, Andrew	126	Grant, John	120
Barton, David	150	Grimsley, William	100
Barton, John	100	Grimsley, Joseph	130
Bennett, Daniel	100	Gudrage, Allen	100
Briggs, William	163	Hamrick, John	134
Brown, Dixon	213	Harris, Samuel	250
Browning, Jacob	100	Hefflin, James	140
Bolt, Robert	200	Hefflin, Simon	200
Burgess, Garner	200	Hume, Andrew	200
Cook, William	800	Heminger, William	105
Corder, William	200	Hitt, Joseph	158
Crim, John, Jr.	100	Humston, John	
Crim, John, Sr.	200	Husht (?), Rosannah	100
Crawley, Richard	200	Jeffrey, George	100
Day, William	200	Jett, John, Sr.	238
Dearing, John	100	Jett, William	100
Devlin, William	200	Jett, James	150
Douglas, Benjamin	130	Jett, Francis	250
Ellis, John	100	Johnston, John	---

Jones, John	170	Oldham, Mary	200
Jones, Charles	200	Pinkard	140
Jones, Henry	100	Priest, John	200
Laurence, Edward	200	Pryor, Benjamin	200
Laurence, Peter	105	Randolph, Richard	150
Littlejohn, Charles	150	Riley, John	200
Linegar, William	118	Settle, George	134
Lovell, Sarah	100	Chumate, John	200
Luttrell, Samuel	150	Sinclair, John	200
Marshall, John	146	Smith, William	200
Marshall, Widow	150	Smith, John	200
McCormack, John	200	Smoot, John	200
McQuin, John	100	Stone, Thomas	250
Morgan, Charles	197	Snelling, Hugh	100
Morgan, William	----	Sudduth, James	128
Murphy, Miles	200	Sullivan, David	--
Neale, Benjamin	200	Swain, Charles	--
Nichols, Samuel	200	Taylor, Charles	120
Norman, Clement	200	Thompson, Jesse	100
Norman, Clement	140	Weaver, Jacob	100
Norman, Jesse	140	Wood, Dickerson	100
Payne, Reuben	200	Waller, Charles	250
Payne, Francis	200	Walker, William	100
Payne, Reuben	140	Welch, David	---
Payne, Thomas	..200	Williams, Joseph	200.
Payne, John	100	Woodyard (Woodard ?), Lewis	200
Pickett, William	275		

A list of fees due Isaac A. Williams, Clerk of Fredericksburg
Chancery Court, in the County of Fauquier, Virginia.
1827

Allen, Henry

Armistead, Robert

Armistead, Ann B.

Armistead, John

Beale, John G.

Bishop, Joshua

Blackwell, Frances

Ball, George

Bogess, Henry

Baylis, John T.

Baylor, Ann D.

Byrne, William

Bayliss, William

Brooke, F.W.

Bruce, Alexander

Chapman, George, Jr.

Chilton, Mark A.

Comly, J.A. & Allen, W.S.

Corbin, James

Cross, James

Crowne, Thomas

Dearing, George

Digges, Edward

Digges, Whiting

Dodd, Ann

Edmonds, William F.

English, James

Fisgback, ---

Farrow, Nimrod

Farrow, Benjamin

Foote, George W.

Foster, Thomas

Floerie, James (or Joseph)

Fitzhugh, Battaile

Frazier, James

Gibson, William

Gillison, -----

Grigsby, Aaron

Grigsby, Nathaniel

Grigsby, Baylis

Gordon, Samuel

Graham, Benjamin

Glascock, Benjamin

Glassell, John

Hart, Robert

Handy, William

Hayes, John

Handy, William

Hayes, John

Haraway, Richard

Hickerson, Elizabeth
Hickerson, Hosea
Hitch, Aquilla
Holtzclaw, Charles
Hume, Robert
Hunton, Thomas
James, David
Jennings, Thomas
Johnson, Turner M.
Kelly, Alexander D.
Kelly, James W.
Kemper, William
Kemper, John
King, Vincent
Latham, George
Latham, Jere D.
Lee, Hancock
Lewis, Henry M.
Martin, George
Maddux, Grover
Mallory, William
Mallory, Edward
Marshall, James M.
McCormick, Stephen
McNeal & Cowles
Moore, Thomas
Murphy, William S.

Murphy, William S.
Obannon, Joseph
Obannon, Benjamin
Obannon, James
Payne, William
Phillips, William F.
Pickett, --------
Poe, William
Porter, John
Richards, Edward D.
Rogers, Notley W.
Rose, Robert H.
Russell, Marcus
Scott, Alexander B.
Shacklett, (?) John
Scott, John
Smith, Walter A.
Shaw, Neale
Smith, Thomas
Smith, William
Smith, Joseph
Strother, Susannah
Strother, John (by next friend)
Strother, Enoch
Sinkler, William (?)
Tutt, Thomas
Triplett, Frances

Murray, William & John	Thompson, Elizabeth
Thornhill, Elijah	Welch, Sylvester
Triplett, William	Withers, Daniel
Turner, Thomas	Hudnal, Mary
Turney, Lewis	Wharton, Samuel
Withers, Jesse	Winn, Jemina
Warde, Berkeley	Weaver, John
Withers, Spencer	Wheatley, James
	Yorby, William G.

(The above list was given merely as an index of the names of some of the families living in Fauquier County in 1827.)

RENT ROLL

PRINCE WILLIAM COUNTY, VIRGINIA

1738

Fauquier County was formed in 1759, being taken from Prince William County, and named after Francis Fauquier, Governor of Virginia.

Many of the following names given on the Rent Roll of Prince William County (1738) are to be found later in Fauquier County.

Arrington, Wansford	Calvert, George, Jr.
Ashmore, Widow	Cummirgs, Malachi
Ash, Francis-	Chapman, Joseph (Heirs)
Abbott, Roger	Champ, Major John
Baker, Charles	Champ, John
Bell, Alexander	Coram, William
Barton, Thomas	Crouch, William
Billings, Jasper	Carr, John
Brooks, Thomas	Cornwell, Charles
Bronaugh, Jeremiah	Crump, John
Bronaugh, Capt. Jeremiah	Corbin, John
Baylis, William	Combs, Emanuel
Bland, John	Combs, Joseph
Buckner, Richard	Compton, William
Berry, Thomas	Chambers, Joseph
Barton, Thomas	Chilton, Capt. Thomas
Buchanan, Joseph, dec'd.	Clemont (Clement), Alexander
Brinbett (?), Henry	Cottonwell, Thomas
Bush, John	Canterbury, John
Calk, James (or Joseph)	Darmott, Michael
Cruppner, Richard	Earle, Samuel

Conyers, Davis
Calvert (or Colvert), George
Calvert, Sarah
French, James
Foster, William
Floyd, Henry
Ficklin, William
Grigg, John
Goslin, John, dec'd.
Graham, Howard
Glascock, John
Garner, John (orphan)
Garner, Thomas
Garner, Vincent
Grant, John (inspector)
Gibson, John, Gent. of N. Carolina
Grubbs, Richard
Grayson, Capt. Benjamin
Harper, George
Hopper, Blagrove
Hopper, John
Hall, Widow
Hancock, Scarlett
Hudnall, Joseph, William & Thos.
Halley, Henry
Hedges, John
Harrison, Thomas

Edy, Samuel
Farrow, John (orphan)
Farrow, William
Johnson, John
Johnson, Jesse
Johnson, Tolito (?)
Kent, ------
Kamper, James
Kamper, John
Kamper, Howson
Kinchloe, John
Linton, Widow
Linton, John
Linton, Moses
Grayson, Benjamin

Ludwell, Philip
Lambert, Hugh
Moss, Mathew
McComkry, Rev. William
Morgan, Charles
Marr, Chris.
Marr, Daniel
Marr, John
Martin, Joseph
Minton, Joseph
McDonald, Donald

Harrison, Burr
Harrison, Thomas, Jr.
Holtzclaw, Jacob & John
Page, John
Routt, William
Russell, William
Strothers, William
Spiller, William
Stone, Thomas
Stribbling, Capt. Thomas
Stamps, Thomas
Smith, William
Sarlson (?), Nicholas
Toward, Orphans
Tackett, Lewis

Nevill, George
Nouman, Widow
Neale, Roswell
Thorn, William
Taylor, Charles
Vicars, Orphans
Veale, Morris
Whitledge, William
Whitledge, Thomas
Whitledge, John
Winwright, John
Wright, Joseph
Wallace, Burr (widow of)
Williams, William
Williams, Jonas

Welch, Thomas

INDEX

Adams, 3, 16, 19, 24, 26, 52, 64
  66, 79, 96, 100, 110

Allen, 4, 17, 19, 21, 37, 41, 51,
  63, 74, 110

Allsup, 15

Alexander, 11, 17, 27, 90

Allison, 29, 72

Ambrose, 5

Amiss, 67

Anderson, 13, 76, 79, 87, 96

Arner, 81

Arnold, 7, 27, 30, 34, 35, 46
  54, 70, 98, 109

Ash, 15, 70, 79, 81

Ashby, 5, 20, 24, 29, 36, 47, 48,
  77, 88, 105, 110, 114

Ashly, 16, 54, 72

Askins, 43

Ashford, 46

Ashmore, 43

Atchinson, 108

Atto_burn, 114

Austin, 104

Babson, 112

Bailoc, 39

Bailey -Baley - 96, 107, 113, 115,

Baley -Bailey, 3, 12, 32, 70

Baker, 26, 71, 106, 109

Ball, 12, 33, 43, 50, 51, 52, 65
  77, 84, 99, 111

Ballard, 24, 39, 45, 92

Balles -Bailes, 28, 105, 69

Banks, 19

Barley, 14

Bannister, 8, 48, 85

Barboe, 55, 62, 72, 83

Barbor, 6, 96, 116

Barbey, 19

Barhan, 26, 27

Barker, 17, 23, 32, 37, 44, 52, 68
  28

Barnes, 77, 91

Barnett, 16, 45, 61

Barr, 79

Barrasks, 72, 30

Barratt, 3, 95

Barrett, 16

Barker, 97, 98, 104

Bartlett, 19, 42, 82

Barton (Barten), 2, 64

Bashaw, 79, 80, 116

Battaly, 36, 114

Batson, 68, 69

Baylis, 41

Baylis, 107

Bayse, 32, 72, 92

Board, 5

Bealo, 53, 89

Beach -Beach, 6, 26

Beckham, 61

Beckwith, 39

Bell, 7, 9, 10, 28, 38, 55

Benjey, 46

Benard, 71

Bencor, 110

Benn, 100

Benson, 79, 106, 107

Bennett, 10, 11

Benum (Denam), 114

Berry, 35

Berryman, 5, 36, 81, 110

Bethel, 98

Bigbie, 98

Birciram, 12

Bird, 70, 94, 106

Billingsby, 105

Bishop, 116

Blackerby, 35

Black, 95

Blackmore, 16

Blackwell, 17, 20, 24, 25, 35, 38, 47, 49, 60, 62, 64, 64, 67, 72, 80, 83, 87, 90, 99, 106, 107, 111

Blackerby, 99, 101

Bland, 32, 44

Blansit, 20

Blithe (Blethe), 103

Bradford, 2, 4, 5, 16, 22, 33, 34, 50, 51, 55, 63, 76, 88, 9 97, 101, 103

Bradley, 44, 50

Brady, 32, 59

Bragg, 38, 77, 78, 80, 105 64.

Brahan, 18

Branan (Brannin) 45, 112, 116

Bramlett, 21, 23, 52.

Brazier, 82

Boggs, 13

Boley, 93

Bollins, 50, 70.

Bordon, 116.

Boscarver, 98.

Bowman, 84, 114

Bowen, 102

Boswell, 82, 85, 95

Bowers 64, 65, 88, 93, 112

Bowmer, 105

Boyd, 20, 26, 81

Brent, 34, 64

Bristraw, 10

Brooks, 1, 7, 12, 46, 54, 56, 57, 67, 80, 95, 97, 99, 104

Bruen, 37

Brown, 4, 5, 22, 29, 39, 40, 45, 46, 49, 54, 56, 62, 65, 78, 80; 85 68, 99, 104, 106, 114

Bronaugh, 21, 55, 67

Bronbaugh, 13, 34, 35, 57, 97

Bronaunt, 30

Browning, 47, 79, 91

Bryan, 30, 74, 104

Bryant, 85

Buchanan, 9, 53, 62

Buckman, 116

Buckner, 37, 49, 112

Burgess, 19, 46, 56, 77, 87, 95, 11

Burdette, 38, 50, 90

Berditt (Burdette), 102

Burger, 87

Burk, 70

Burnett, 38

Burrough, 111

Butcher, 111

Bullitt, 1, 8, 26, 42, 49

Bussey, 64, 65

Butler, 3, 5, 6, 26, 30, 33, 42, 46

Butcher, 111

Button, 2, 112

Cain, 54

Calmes, 16

Calvert, 62

Calvin, 91

Campbell, 78, 98

Carroll, 70

Carter, 41, 50, 54, 85, 117

Carle, 19

Carr, 26

Carpenter, 14, 40, 47, 64

Carvell, 19, 27

Catlett, 21, 44

Cave, 59, 63

Cavanaugh, 45, 91, 111

Chadwell, 59

Chamberlain, 35, 80, 96, 106

Channell, 61

Channell, 61

Chapman, 26

Chapwell, 92

Chester, 62

Chichester, 12, 16

Chilton, 16, 17, 20, 27, 36, 41, 43, 46, 56, 62, 64, 67, 110

Chinn, 43, 53, 65, 102, 83, 107, 114, 116

Chirley, 82

Coppedge (Coppage), 7, 14, 15, 21, 27, 44, 49, 54

Chunn, 18, 24, 28, 72

Claggett, 65

Clark, 27, 48, 50, 58

Claypool, 78

Clemans, 108

Cleveland, 109

Clement, 17, 57

Clendenning, 81, 108

Clifton, 24

Climan, 103

Cockran-Cockrin, 33, 50, 62

Cockrell, 18, 33, 48, 95, 96

Colvert, 88

Collins, 42, 87, 91, 93

Collier, 7

Colvin, 76

Combs, 8, 20, 24, 29, 60, 79

Congrove, 114

Constable, 93, 104

Conway, 8, 33, 38, 65

Conway, 1, 10, 22, 26, 32, 34, 41, 42, 49, 67, 68, 74

Coodnick, 96

Cook, 31, 48, 49. 57, 78, 95, 106

Cooksey, 59

Cooper, 84, 94

Cunningham., 61

Corbin, 16

Corder, 4, 85, 87, 115

Corum (Coram), 7, 20

Cornwell, 18, 25, 70, 91

Cornelius, 10, 94

Conway, 79, 86, 94

Cox, 62, 69, 90

Crafford, 98

Craig, 11, 31, 33, 34, 66, 98

Cramp, 19

Crawford, 94

Crawley, 81

Crook, 78

Crees, 99

Cremoh, 79

Crockett, 36, 91

Crosby, 30, 41, 48, 88, 102, 114

Crosley, 47

Croudh, 88

Cross, 65

Crump, 4, 45, 91, 98, 102, 114

Crum-Crump, 60, 80

Crupper, 58. 114

Cummings, 12, 31, 33 -Cummins, 87

Cundiffe, 64

Dixon, 85

Curtis, 71, 78, 108

Cusenberry (Quisenberry), 95

Dade, 29

Dareing, 43

Dairs, 78, 82, 115

Dale, 73

Darnall, 3, 4, 8, 12, 19, 21, 25
    28, 42, 52, 54,. 65, 105,
    108, 110, 115

Davenport, 5

Davidson, 98

Davis, 21, 54, 59, 61, 65, 78, 110

Dawson, 51, 111

Day, 49, 52, 66

Deal, 91

Deane, 12

Dearon, 86

Dearing, 50, 114

Debell, 112.

Delgram, 21

Delaney, 19

Dennison, 92

Dennis, 53, 57, 65

Dermont, 82

Dickman, 59

Degges-Digges, 59, 63, 67

Divis (Davis), 55

Dobie-Diby, 31, 66

Dodd, 26, 36, 102, 110

Dodson, 10, 19, 20

Doleas, 112

Donaldson. 21, 22

Donphan, 74

Doty, 94

Douglas, 98

Doutman, 107

Dowell, 100

Downing, 89

Downs, 58

Dowdall, 21

Drummond, 21, 34, 54, 98, 117

Duff, 26, 87

Duffy, 61, 63

Dugarde, 18, 22

Dulaney, 51

Dulin, 4, 50, 66, 96, 104

Duncan, 2, 21, 37, 51, 52, 57, 59
    78, 80, 86, 87, 90, 91, 92,
    93, 99, 102, 106, 116, 115

Dye, 91

Dyson, 72

Earle, 5

Eastham- Esthane, 63

Eaton, 79

Edge, 12, 34

Edmonds, 5, 11, 13, 21, 37, 41, 41, 55, 63, 78, 81, 87, 91, 95

Edmonson, 95

Edrington, 12

Edwards, 4, 8, 13, 27, 46, 63

Elgin, 94

Elias, 69

Elliott, 40, 87, 106

Ellott-Elliott, 11, 15, 28, 30, 84, 102, 112, 114

Ellen, 94

Ellis, 25, 70, 82, 106

Embry, 45, 46, 84, 99, 100, 112, 113

Emmins- Emmons, 57

Eskridge, 24

Etheson, 109

Ethrington, 21

Eustaces, 45, 53, 58, 65, 88, 90, 97, 99

Evans, 17, 40, 54, 80, 116

Fanboon -Fanbin, 13, 81

Farrow, 47, 48, 91, 98

Feagan-Feagin, 27, 47, 64, 79, 85

Fenner, 52

Ferguson, 51

Fever, 33

Fuller, 84

French, 33, 43, 113

Fidler (Pedler) 93

Fields, 20, 32, 40, 106

Fielding, 36, 84

Finnie, 4, 22

Finch, 62, 108, 115

Fisher, 51, 97

Fishback, 3, 29, 37, 38, 42, 45, 48, 51, 59, 60, 73, 84, 100

Fitzhugh, 42, 47, 60, 73

Florence, 97, 104

Fletcher, 2, 36, 51, 56, 77, 86, 112

Fleming, 23

Flowerees, 4

Flynn, 56

Foley, 86, 97, 114, 54

Foote, 2, 7, 11, 17, 23, 27, 87, 101, 113

Ford, 31, 114

Forrister-Forrester, 54

Foster, 88, 108

Fowkes, 15, 29, 30, 99, 102, 105, 108, 110

Fowler, 33

Fox, 53, 54

Frazier, 34

Freeman, 10, 42, 48, 57, 76, 86, 88, 92, 111

Frie-Frye, 102, 113

Greenwood, 53

Gregory, 109

Furr, 33, 64, 76, 89

Garner, 33, 36, 37, 46, 56, 68, 87

Gavner, 109

Gear, 52

Gellerson-Gillison, 69

George, 22, 25, 58, 60, 82

Goum, 43

Gibson, 1, 8, 14, 15, 23, 38, 47, 49, 53, 60, 63, 65, 80, 94, 99

Gillison, 14, 38, 62, 80, 86, 87

Gilbert, 17

Giles, 84, 88

Glass, 36

Glasscock, 34, 37, 62, 66, 78, 84, 86, 90. 101, 102, 103, 108

Goldsmith, 56

Gore, 112

Gough, 81

Goodin, 88

Graham, 115

Grant, 22, 25, 36, 38, 39, 57, 70, 80, 90, 91, 96, 98, 99, 102

Graves, 37

Gray, 41

Gre.n, 7, 41, 47, 70, 90, 101, 106, 107

Greening, 83

Griffin, 60, 110, 116

Grinnan, 55, 95, 111

Grigsby, 29, 44, 99, 92, 104, 111, 113, 114

Griffith, 26, 35, 56

Grogan, 27

Guthrie, 26

Guthrie - Guthridge, 69, 83

Guy, 93, 95

Hackley, 48, 64

Haddock, 32

Haddrick-Heddtick, 104

Hainey, 82

Haley, 45, 82

Hall, 3, 16, 80, 98, 105, 111 (19)

Hamilton, 43, 44, 97

Hampton, 9, 12, 16, 45, 69, 71 68, 80, 101, 110, 112

Hambucks, 25

Hamrick, 10, 28

Hanson, 65, 112

Hanor, 50

Hansborough, 18, 66 92

Hardin3, 6, 7, 84, 115

Harley, 89

Hardeween, 17

Hardiwick, 98, 102

Hardistree, 61

Harper, 95, 110

Harris, 37, 45, 55, 56, 58, 65
92, 93, 100

Harrison, 14, 16, 20, 23, 44, 47
59, 60, 87, 88, 92, 100

Harrill, 34, 83

Hathaway -Hathway, 18, 25, 30, 28,
42, 90, 92, 102, 104

Hawkins, 83

Hayes, 83, 84, 90

Haynes, 34

Haynie, 10

Haydon, 41

Haslerigg, 41

Heale, 82, 101

Headley, 49

Healey, 43

Hedengran, 12

Heffering, 51

Hefflin, 74, 76, 80, 92

Hefferling, 92

Helms, 16, 17, 38, 58

Henlon, 92

Hennie, 14

Hendley, 37

Henton (Hinton), 28

Hendren, 34

Henry, 87, 90, 103

Henson, 90

Henderson, 114

Henslee, 90

Herring, 90, 99

Hich, 40

Hickson, 84

Hichlhorn, 108

Hickman, 103, 111, 28

Hilburn, 86

Hill, 52, 102, 113

Hilkin, 93

Hinson, 67, 82, 86

Hitch, 76, 79, 111

Hite, 5

Hitt, 3, 13, 22, 25, 70, 78, 90
94, 101

Hickinson, 78, 87

Hockman, 45

Hogan, 103, 111, 21

Hogin -Hogan, 9, 21

Home, 6, 86, 87

Holmes, 21, 36, 80

Holder, 84

Holiday, 31, 66

Holton, 31, 104

Holly, 108

Holtzclaw, 2, 3, 10, 37, 94, 99,
104.

Holder, 84

Hooes, 63

Hopper, 4

Hopwood, 94, 100

Hord, 81, 94

Horner, 65

Horton, 17, 97, 103

Howell, 81, 100

Hudnall, 23, 83, 85, 115

Hudson, 84

Huffman, 79

Hughes, 11, 100

Hulett, 32

Hume, 21, 22, 68, 84, 94, 96, 106, 111

Humston, 5, 16, 58, 93

Hummins, 92

Hurst, 51

Jacob, 115

Jackman, 3, 30, 31, 62 - 45

Jackson, 13, 34, 37, 59, 96, 110

James, 4, 19, 21, 22, 23, 31, 47, 57, 68, 71, 74, 86, 87, 78, 95, 106, 107

Jameson, 69

Jannaway, 74

Jeffries, 47, 64, 82, 89, 97, 109

Jenkins, 37, 85, 110

Jenny, 106

Jennings, 21, 22, 37, 42, 58, 86, 116

Jett, 3, 10, 92, 108, 109

Joiner, 34

Jones, 14, 16, 33, 36, 41, 57, 65, 66, 77, 88, 91, 93, 94, 103, 111, 112, 113

Johnson, 2, 10, 13, 17, 23, 31, 33, 49, 50, 58, 60, 79, 85, 96, 104, 105, 106

Johnston, 5, 45, 70, 98, 104

Kamper, 2, 3, 9, 42, 72, 98, 99

Kearns, 85

Kearton, 71

Keating, 61

Keen, 53

Keith, 20, 24, 35, 42, 43, 44, 57, 58, 64, 91

Kelly, 36, 99

Kemper, 81, 97, 99, 101, 102

Kemp, 101

Kenard, 23, 61, 92

Kendall, 80, 103

Kennady, 98, 107

Kenton, 35, 42

Kenner, 24, 32, 39, 42, 62, 100, 108, 109

Kerrs, 22, 36, 51, 54, 57, 60, 68, 105

Keyes, 24, 31, 78, 83, 84

Kidwell, 54, 86, 111

Kibble, 98
Kinchloe, 10, 17, 25, 32, 90
King, 12, 64, 65, 70
Kines, 56
Kirk, 28, 106
Kish, 86
Lacy, 68
Luke, 79
Lansdown, 44
Lambert, 65
Lampkin, 105, 110
Lane, 10
Lathane, 45, 89
Latham, 89
Laurance, 78, 80
Lawerence, 1, 7, 10, 25, 54, 40, 41, 88, 98, 106, 109
Lawson, 17, 41, 42, 52, 59, 66
Lawler, 40, 112
Laws, 64
Leach, 45, 76, 82, 94, 109, 114
Leachman, 115
Leake, 79
Lee, 35, 46, 59, 98
Lear (or Sear), 12, 42, 76
Lewis, 19, 21, 22, 45, 67, 68, 84, 98
Linn, 80
Linton, 105

Little, 94
Leake, 98
Lee, 107
Loman, 4
Lombard, 69
Lowe, 87
Lowry, 103
Lunce, 79
Lunceford, 32, 78
Luckett, 63
Luttrell, 7, 9, 19, 20, 23, 24, 29, 34, 41, 101
Luntford. ----
Lynn, 52
Maddox – Maddux, 13, 23, 33, 16, 85
Mahoney, 103

Mallory, 57, 61, 72, 103
Manly, 22
Manrony, 1
Manuel, 50
Marr, 4, 22, 37
Markham, 1, 10, 22
Martin, 3, 25, 39, 41, 43, 50, 51, 54
Marshall, 1, 3, 4, 8, 16, 26, 31, 35, 95, 103, 104
Mason, 41, 53, 116
Masters, 39, 90
Mathews, 80, 87, 108
Mathis, 10

Mauzy, 10, 34, 47, 51, 59, 72, 74, 77, 82
May, 44, 77
McBee, 77, 86
McCarty, 41
McClan, 10
McCormack, 10, 76
McCormick, 2, 41, 76, 86, 92
McChesney, 33
McClanahan, 83, 99, 107, 108, 111
McDaniel, 4
McEndrees, 62
McFarland, 68, 82
McKay, McCay, 37, 89, 104
McKenny, 54, 80, 88
McKensy, 23
McKonkey, 76
McObcy (McAvoy,), 32
McQueen, 110
McTeavor, 102
McVeagh, 68
Metcalf, 12, 30, 32, 35, 52, 58, 59, 61, 101
Michael, 112
Miller, 76, 96
Millar, 3, 11, 39
Millard, 31

Minter, 13, 16, 20, 78, 115
Miskel, 24
Mitchell, 38
Moffett, 15, 18, 31, 33, 88, 91, 115
Monroe, 31, 33, 52, 69, 76, 85, 92
Montgomery, 49
Monday, 85
Morgan, 7, 8, 13, 14, 30, 34, 44, 50, 52, 66, 88, 89, 99, 100
Moore, 9, 58, 83, 114
Morehead, 9, 10, 12, 25, 26, 28, 32, 38, 41, 43, 50, 58, 67, 86, 92, 100, 104, 106, 107, 113
Moreland, 79
Morris, 103, 33
Morrison, 28
Moss, 21, 63, 112
Mossless (?), 6
Mumsey, 32
Murphy, 44, 74, 97
Murray, 7, 20, 28, 33, 40, 43, 48, 70, 104, 109, 110
Mycratt, 12
Nalle, 39
Neale, 19, 25, 38, 40, 46, 53, 57, 73, 89, 100, 101, 109, 47
Nelson, 18, 22, 25, 38, 44, 40, 48, 76, 95, 115
Nevill, 9, 15, 16, 30, 93, 95

N eigh, 60

Newean, 4

Newby, 49

Newhouse, 95

Newport, 93

Newstead, 82

Newell, 31

Norman, 3, 40, 49

Norris, 22, 27, 66, 68, 71

Nugent, 39, 45

Nutt, 69

Obannon, 5, 11, 15, 21, 23, (19)
58, 59, 69, 84, 96, 98,
103, 104

Oar, 89

Odor, 96

Oglsby, 88

Oldacres, 53, 78, 79, 86

Oliver, 115

Orear, 63

Owens, 20, 35, 56, 104

Owing, 50

Page, 4

Palmer, 81, 101

Parker, 4, 8, 9, 17, 25, 40, 44,
58, 81, 95

Parklow, 79

Parlow, 48

Parr, 51

PATTIE, 133

Payne, 32, 88, 90, 91, 102, 106,
11, 112

Pearce, 34

Peake, 22, 27, 28

Pearse, 12, 34

Pearl, 40, 48, 58

Pearson, 98

Pendleton, 66

Pepper-Peper, 48, 50, 76, 87

Perry, 9, 105

Peters, 15, 28, 29, 63, 67, 84, 117

Peyton, 5, 29, 45, 54, 59, 96

Phillips, 30, 76, 79, 82, 108

Pickett, 8, 20, 25, 32, 42, 59, 67,
68, 72, 89, 93, 95, 100, 101,
110

Pickard, 88

Pinkard, 65, 103

Piper, 32

Pinkstone, 108

Pitcher, 32

Pope, 21, 24

Porter, 3, 48, 50, 62, 63, 71, 76,
82, 105, 106, 116

Powell, 67

Pragh, 89, 109

Prall, 98

Pranor, 89

Preston, 5, 12

Parson, 83

Priest, 9, 28, 39, 41, 54, 85, 98

Pritchett, 4

Putnam, 107

Quarles, 14, 95

Queens, 98

Quisenberry, 51, 68

Railey-Raley, 20, 83

Rakestraw, 93

Ralls, 18

Ransdell, 7, 18, 36, 41, 57, 60
 83, 90, 106

Randall, 112

Randolph, 113

Ranson, 1, 9, 10, 34

Ratcliffe, 88

Rawlins, 52

Read, 101

Ready, 49

Reaves, 36

Reading, 5, 6

Rector, 2, 13, 22, 30, 37, 44, 62,
 68, 83, 84, 90, 26, 107, 113, 93

Reed, 64, 111

Redd, 76

Reddin, 4, 50

Redman, 1, 9, 56

Rennolds, 18

Preston, 5, 12

Rennolds, 18

Roynolds, 35

Richard, 1

Riddle, 76

Ridley, 44

Riley, 42, 52, 87, 91, 95, 114

Rhodes, 86

Roach, 22, 43

Robert, 91, 107

Robinson, 22, 31, 32, 39, 68, 77, 82,
 89, 92, 101, 108, 116

Roberson, 12, 22, 28

Robertson, 26, 64

Rogers, 5, 12, 20, 49, 53, 57, 69,
 100, 109, 114, 113

Roe, 102

Roizer, 103

Rollins, 113

Roley, Roby, 97

Roper, 33, 116

Rose, 72, 116

Rosser, 16, 101, 116

Rossean, 60, 106

Routt, 44, 48, 78, 82, 93, 106

Rookhard, 62

Russell, 2, 3, 21, 22, 23, 54, 97,
 103, 111

Rust, 22, 87

Ryan, 74

Sanders, 12, 40, 46, 49, 81

Sanford, 61

Scott, 11, 16, 21, 29, 40, 41, 42, 45, 62, 69

Seaton, 7, 24, 32, 33, 35, 49, 56, 62, 70, 109, 115

Seaman, 6, 9, 42

Selden, 62

Settle, 13, 18, 27, 30, 43, 46, 54, 82, 85, 89, 96, 115, 117

Shacklatt, 67

Shackleford, 6, 17, 46, 55, 90, 101

Shadrack, 2

Shadwell, 81

Shark, 92

Sharp, Sharpe, 39, 45, 89, 115

Slaver, 96

Sheets, 53

Shehogan, 92

Shipps, 21, 79, 81

Shirley, Shurley, 16, 20

Shud, 86

Shumate, 15, 19, 20, 36, 38, 41, 45, 56, 62, 68, 78, 89, 94, 100, 104, 115

Sia_, 26

Simmons, 81

Simpson, 110

Sinclair, 11, 12, 54, 79

Singer, 81

Sinkler, 9, 18, 61, 87

Singleton, 52, 100, 117

Silliman-Siliman, 4, 48

Skinner, 44, 67

Slaughter, 41, 72, 101

Smith, 1, 5, 6, 19, 22, 23, 30, 31, 33, 40, 50, 54, 57, 58, 59, 60, 66, 67, (69,) 77, 78, 81, 82, 83, 85, 88, 89, 90, 99, 100, 104, 106 107, 111

Smoot, 96, 104

Smooth, 58, 59, 70

Snelling, 16, 46, 76, 113

Snyder, 100, 106

Southard, 11, 21

Soddust, 60

Spenny, 68

Spicer, 110

Spiller-Spilla, 59, 112

Spillman, 30

Squires, 27, 118

Stadler, 68

Stanton, 109

Stamps, 6, 12, 100

Starke, 4, 28, 90, 94, 105

Steard- Steatard, 49

Steele, 45, 57, 68, 81

Stiggens-Steggens, 101

Stigler, 64, 71, 87

Stephens, 11, 14, 54, 74, 87, 93

Stephenson, 52

Stevinson, 52, 96, 112

Stewart, 1, 10, 26, 29, 30, 43, 63, 66, 107

Stinson, 88

Stone, 2, 11, 30, 47, 84, 101

Stringfellow, 76, 79, 81

Strother, 25, 40, 61, 65, 90, 105, 106

Sudduth, 30, 31

Suttard, 25

Suttle, 38, 56, 76

Summers, 21

Sullivan, 35, 61, 84, 84, 109

Tackett, 6

Taits, 29

Taylor, 2, 4, 9, 13, 22, 27, 36, 44, 46, 53, 79, 89, 91, 95, 103, 110

Talbot, 57, 58

Taliaferrio, 112

Tapp, 83

Tarlton, 112, 113

Teagle, 113

Tebbs, 97

Tebbetts, 97

Telling, 102

Tennell, 2

Tennison, 99

Tharp, 71

Thatcher, 34

Thomas, 61, 82, 84, 92, 97, 110

Thornton, 58

Thompson, 51, 93, 104, 109, 115

Throckmorton, 46

Thornberry, 62, 102, 115

Thorndyke, 89

Thornhill, 39, 40

Threlkeld, 1, 3

Tibbs, 74, 79

Tiffin, 106

Timberlake, 49, 65, 68

Toff, 93

Tomkils, 46

Tompkins, 68

Tomson, 104

Toll - Tolle, 23, 27, 48, 95

Tongue, 63

Townsend, 39

Tidler, 25

Traverse, 74

Triplett, 52, 53, 83, 91, 112, 113

Tupman, 11

Turberville, 32

Turley -Turty, 114, 116

Tullos, 97

Turner, 26, 27, 28, 51, 72, 76, 78, 83, 103, 109

Tyler, 9,

Twentymen, 3,

Utterback, 30, 44, 45, 54, 64, 103

Underwood, 1, 30, 64

Vanderbilt, 98

Vaughn, 89

Waddell, 44, 102, 114, 116

Waddle, 70

Wagner, 57

White, 53

Wake, 71,

Walker, 62, 67, 79, 85

Walls, 11, 13

Walters, 33, 74, 77

Walton, 74

Warden, 68

Watkins, 88

Watters, 59

Watts, 23, 58, 74, 92

Waugh, 34, 45, 74

Weadon, 40

Weaver, 3, 90

Weakley, 8

Weeks -Weaks, 101

Weathers (Withers), 23

Wells, 85

Weeden, 57, 113

Wellborn, 2

Welch, 19, 96, 102

Westfall, 45

West, 50, 53, 114

Wharton, 48

Wheatley, 31, 33, 66, 88, 94, 99

Whitley, 22, 85, 92

Whitacre, 93

White, 11, 23, 39, 43, 77, 95, 107, 117

Whiting, 31, 73, 86

Wicks, 41

Wickliffe, 32, 56, 86, 101

Wigginton, 37, 63

Williamson, 16, 37

Willis, 31, 101

Winn, 33, 53, 69, 110

 Williams, 7, 9, 30, 33, 37, 41, 42, 48, 52

Wilson, 81, 89, 108

Winterton, 81

Wisheve, 103

Withers, 36, 37, 41, 45, 46, 47, 48, 51, 55, 56, 60, 71, 74, 78, 83, 85, 89, 96, 114, 115, 116

Wood, 6, 8, 20, 59, 68, 70, 82, 95, 116

Woodford, 40, 49

Webb, 24

Wolf, 106

Wright, 3, 12, 19, 21, 30, 32,
    48, 68, 76, 80, 87, 95, 96.
    110

Woodyard - Woodward, 31, 78

Wren - Wrenn, 51, 89, 114

Wyatt, 45

Young, 9, 21, 24, 29, 31, 89

www.ingramcontent.com/pod-product-compliance
Lightning Source LLC
LaVergne TN
LVHW091549060526
838200LV00036B/765